All rights reserved.

No part of this publication may be re
transmitted in any form or by any means, without
permission from the author.

Copyright: Ian Cook 2021

Edition 2.0

Front Cover: CP 1423 at Porto Campanha with the ECS from Porto Sao Bento after earlier working the 06.24 from Penafiel on the 18th April 1996.

Back Cover: CP 1803 at Barreiro station prior to working the 16.40 Barreiro to Praias-Sado on the 19th April 1996.

I dedicate this book to my daughters, Lisa and Stephanie, who mean the world to me. In addition, I would also like to dedicate this book to my friend Brian Horn, who recently passed away whilst I was writing this book. Brian was the person responsible for appointing me to my first job at Manchester Polytechnic, which later became The Manchester Metropolitan University.

All Photographs contained in this book are owned and were taken by Ian Cook (The Author), unless otherwise stated.

Content   Pages

1. Introduction.   4 - 11
2. The End of Type 2's on Passenger Services in Scotland.   12 - 24
3. Crompton Diesels.   25 - 33
4. Cambrian Coast holiday Services.   34 - 38
5. Summer Services in the 1980s.   39 - 44
6. Railtours and Special Events.   45 - 53
7. Portugal.   54 - 90
8. The Republic of Ireland.   91 - 108
9. Belgium.   109 - 146
10. Germany and the European Report.   147 - 179

1 - Introduction

With my first book "Recollections of a Train Spotter in the 1960s" published and the fact that we are still in a Covid lockdown, I decided it's time to press on and start my second book. The first covered the period from approximately 1963 to 1984, so it seems appropriate to continue roughly where I left off. By the mid 1980's I was firmly into the hobby of Bashing, which is when a railway enthusiast prefers to actually ride behind a locomotive rather than just sit down at a station writing down an endless list of train numbers. The one immediate benefit of Bashing is that you see a lot more of the railway system and the actual country itself. I suspect I really started Bashing around the time the Deltics started to be withdrawn from service. In the final two years of the Deltics i.e., 1979 to 1980, I usually took a week off work around the summer bank holiday and purchased an East Midlands weekly Rover Ticket. This ticket included New Mills close to where I lived and an area covering Sheffield, Doncaster, Cleethorpes, Skegness, Peterborough, Leicester, Derby and back to New Mills. The ticket allowed an individual unrestricted journeys within the area covered by the ticket, which also allowed you to ride behind the Deltics on the East Coast Main Line (ECML) from Doncaster down to Peterborough. In addition, I would travel over to Skegness to take advantage of the holiday services that provided the public the chance of a holiday on the East Coast of England, these trains were frequently hauled by engines that would usually be hauling freight trains. For example, Class 20s would usually be used to haul coal trains in the East Midlands but these services were considerably reduced during the summer months, when the Power Stations didn't use as much coal. This allowed the authorities to take advantage of a variety of diesels including Class 20s, 31s, 37s and 47s to haul some of the additional services provided to get holiday makers from their homes in places like: Sheffield, Derby, Chesterfield, Leicester, Nottingham and further afield like Liverpool, Manchester and Birmingham, to places like Skegness and Yarmouth. A similar arrangement occurred on the West Coast with summer services being provided to: Llandudno, Blackpool, Southport as well as places in Mid Wales i.e., Aberystwyth, Pwllheli, Barmouth and Porthmadog.

During this time the interest in the railways with regard to haulage completely took off and resulted in thousands of enthusiasts enjoying this relatively new way of being a railway enthusiast. Bashing wasn't just an interest for the younger enthusiast but included men up to and including retirement age. The hobby even attracted a small number of women but most would only be involved due to their boyfriend or partners interest in the hobby.

It didn't take long before you gained a huge circle of friends, who were all into the world of haulage and would frequently meet up to chase after locomotives that involved travel all over the country. In the North West of England, I knew around 50 or more friends who regularly spent most weekends, especially during the summer travelling all of the country in pursuit of their hobby. In addition, you soon got to know groups of other enthusiasts from areas outside your own particular location who would be totally focused on the hobby.

The most important thing to Bashers, in those days was getting hold of the information to what certain classes of locomotives were working on passenger services, the rarer the locomotive the more interesting they would be to bashers. In addition, certain classes of locomotives gained huge followings and their followers would concentrate all their efforts chasing only their preferred class of locomotives. Early examples of this would include the diesel hydraulic class 'The Westerns' and eventually classes such as the Deltics and Class Forties.

The information was referred to as 'Gen' and usually resulted in thousands of 'phone calls across the country when the 'Gen' was distributed to those who regularly ventured all over the country in pursuit of their hobby. This was in the days before mobile 'phones and was certainly before the Internet surfaced, so no Social Media to help distribute the 'Gen'. By the mid 1980's I would regularly get a 'phone call early on a summer Saturday morning with an extensive list of those trains that had been allocated an engine that would be viewed as interesting to Bashers. British Railways at this time had introduced a computer system which logged and managed the operation of all the locomotives assets, it was known as 'TOPS' (Total Operations Processing System), which was designed to allow them to manage their locomotives and eventually other assets including coaches, wagons etc. Fortunately, a few individuals also had access to this information, which allowed the gen to be gathered on what was working on a passenger service at any particular moment in time. Certain workings would be a priority including many of the summer holiday workings for example the Cambrian Coast holiday trains, Skegness and Yarmouth holiday trains, plus dozens of other services covering holiday destinations such as on the South Coast i.e., Bournemouth, Weymouth, Penzance, Tenby to name a few. The list of interesting workings usually covered several sides of A4 paper, once I had received the 'Gen', it was my task to then pass this onto another group of friends, who in turn would also pass it onto their own group of friends. A bit like Pyramid distribution and it certainly worked and by 06.00 am I would be formulating a plan to get as many of the locomotives that you could possibly get to in one day. In addition, you frequently worked hand in hand with close friends to achieve your objective. Then it was, get showered, dressed and pack your bag for the days adventure, which could well involve travelling hundreds of miles. Not one day would be like another and would be totally dictated by the locomotives that would be working. A good example of this was during 1985 when I would join Steve Kemp and a few other friends for a fast car journey over to Sheffield where we were able to get a further update on the 'Gen' from a fellow enthusiast who had access to the latest TOPS information. We would then usually cover the diesel on the Sheffield to Blackpool service then back in the car for a fast journey down to Long Eaton to pick up a number of the Class 20s on holiday services heading to Skegness. Then back in the car for another fast car move over to Shrewsbury, to cover some of the services that were working the Cambrian coast that day. To a person who has no interest in railways, this may sound a little strange but it was the most productive way of covering as many of the engines that were of interest to you that had been allocated to work.

Another useful aid that appeared in the 1980's, was the Platform 5 publication 'Loco-Hauled Travel' book series originally credited to Neil Webster and by 1984 was credited to Neil Webster and my friends Simon Greaves and Robert Greengrass and published by Metro Enterprises Ltd. The book detailed the diagrams for most diesel and electric classes that worked passenger services. The first copy I have of the book covered the period 1982-1983 and included a few examples of bashing Itineraries. The edition for the period 1985-1986 was the first to include the diagrams of the Class 37s on the Cambrian Coast during the summer.

Loco-Hauled Travel 1985-1986

Another aspect of this new world of Bashing was the language used by individuals, which became commonly used across the entire country. First of all, many classes of locomotives acquired nicknames, some classes even attracted numerous nicknames, Class 47s were called Duffs, Spoons, Joeys and few other unpleasant names, owing to the class being about the most common diesel locomotive you would find hauling passenger trains. In addition, to nicknames modern rail enthusiasts would use a language during their conversations with fellow enthusiasts, which included names for elderly people i.e., Bert and Ada or 'Normals' for general members of the public, whereas young females were referred to as 'Baglets'. Tickets were referred to as pieces, cost of tickets or change would be called

'Ching'! Guards and Ticket Inspectors were referred to as 'Grippers' and many TTI (Travelling Ticket Inspectors) got nicknames of their own i.e., Goldilocks etc. Travelling without a legitimate ticket was called 'Effing' and sometimes involved individuals hiding in a toilet on a train to avoid paying for a ticket. Needing sleep is referred to as 'Doss' and the word 'Dreadful' was often used to confirm something good, as was the comment 'My Lords'! The list is endless!

In addition, to the strange language used, many Bashers would try their best to avoid paying for accommodation and would prefer to travel on an overnight service rather than stay in a B&B or hotel. Obviously, this resulted in certain individuals starting to look more like tramps as their appearance steadily got worse during a long trip. I remember, individuals who spent weeks in Scotland would take a tent with them to minimise the cost of the trip. One individual, who I won't name went to sleep on a platform at Leipzig HBF, with the intention of doing an overnight, once it arrived. Unfortunately, the overnight arrived and departed with the individual still asleep on the platform bench!!

Finally, whilst travelling behind their preferred motive power, bashers would tend to occupy the coaches closest to the locomotive for the full-on audio effects of the locomotive. This was usually combined with them hanging out of the windows of the front coaches waving their arms about in a movement referred to as 'Aeroplaning'.

An example of Bashers 'Aeroplaning' in the front coach behind 40085 working the 08.05 Manchester Pic to Skegness on 13th August 1983. Not my photograph and was taken by a former work colleague who unfortunately, I can't remember his name.

Obviously, the authorities didn't like to see people hanging out of the windows of their trains and tried to prevent this by inserting a pin in the window frame to prevent them from opening. This was commonly applied to the coaches used on railtours. Solution, take your own pliers and screwdriver to remove the said pin, allowing the window to open again. Which would be greatly appreciated on hot summers days allowing fresh air into the coach. Obviously, this was just an idea, not as if anyone would even consider undertaking such a reckless act.

2 - The end of Type 2's in Scotland on Passenger Services

As detailed in my first book, my hobby gradually involved being away from home for up to a week, the first of these being my trip to Scotland during September 1985 when I travelled up to Scotland on the evening of the 22nd September and returned home on the 29th September. This was the first time I had ever stayed away from home for even just one night. It was around this time that it became known that ScotRail intended to eliminate the use of the small Type 2 diesels used on any of their passenger services by the end of September 1986. Consequently, I decided to spend more time in Scotland covering these workings before it was too late.

My next opportunity occurred when I attended a conference at Edinburgh University, which I extended the visit to include a stay at my usual B&B in Haymarket. I travelled up to Scotland on the 7th January 1986 and returned home on the 11th Jan 1986, during which time I spent a couple of days covering the services on the Edinburgh to Dundee and Perth routes. The highlight of the trip was on the 11th January the last day of the trip, when I dropped on 20203 hauling a very poorly 27051 whilst working the 09.30 Dundee to Waverley service. Rescuing failed passenger engines was about the only way you could hope to have a Scottish based Class 20 north of border on a passenger service.

20203 and 27051 at Edinburgh Waverley after arriving with the 09.30 from Dundee on the 11th January 1986.

Another memory I have of the trip was one evening I was waiting at Inverkeithing for a service from Dundee to arrive and a DMU arrived in place of the booked diesel, which I took back to Waverley. Soon after leaving Inverkeithing the Guard came to me and checked my ticket and asked if I had seen an elderly man get on the train, to which I replied I hadn't. The Guard then tried to find the elderly gentlemen without any success but as we arrived at Waverley the Elderly man (in his 80's) just stepped off the train onto the platform and was immediately challenged by the Guard. Apparently, the old man had hidden under one of the double seats to avoid paying for a ticket which even took the Guard by surprise.

27037 waits to depart Inverkeithing with the 12.15 Edinburgh to Dundee service on the 11th January 1986.

My next trip to Scotland didn't take place until the 20th August returning home on the 27th August 1986. This trip coincided with a dispute at Haymarket depot involving the maintenance engineers who were working to rule, resulting in many DMU services being replaced by Class 26 diesels hauling rakes of very old dilapidated Mk 1 coaches. This was an opportunity not to be missed and resulted in huge numbers of enthusiasts descending on Scotland. Unfortunately, this trip coincided with the Edinburgh Festival resulting in me being unable to get into my usual B&B in Haymarket and I was forced to stay at a B&B in Inverkeithing. When I arrived at the B&B I was welcomed by an elderly lady who looked like Bette Davis. She escorted me to my room and told me there were no keys for the room doors, which was alarming to say the least. To stop the door lock operating she had stuffed paper into the door recess, which was even more weird. Anyhow I didn't do anything more about it until I settled down for the night and promptly removed the paper from the recess, so the door lock could operate and I slept well. In the morning, I had forgotten about the door lock issues and fortunately went to the shared bathroom in my jeans to have my shower and freshen up. On returning to my bedroom, I was unable to get into my room as the door was locked. So, I went down to see the landlady to ask for the key, to which replied 'You don't need a key as the locks don't operate', wrong 'mine does' as I unpicked the paper from the door recess, to which she replied 'That wasn't a clever thing to do was it!'. After sitting around for what appeared an eternity she asked if I had left my Bedroom Window open, which thankfully I had. So, to get back into my room, I had to climb onto an external wall, then walk along the top of the wall onto the roof of kitchen extension. Then a walk across the top of the Kitchen extension before I climbed into my room via the open sash window. Whilst this was going on, I was being watched by a few neighbours who must have wondered what on earth was going on, I'm surprised the Police didn't arrive and start asking awkward questions. Once back in my room, I immediately replaced the paper back into the recess to stop the lock operating, lesson learnt the hard way!

That evening after completing my days bashing, I decided to pay a visit to one of the local Fish and Chip shops close to where I was staying. After asking for a Scottish Pie Supper, the guy simply threw my pie into the deep-frying fat to warm it up, which didn't impress me one iota! I asked him if I could have a pie that wasn't deep fried and dripping in oil, to which the reply was 'No'! So, no more Scottish Pie Suppers during that trip. At the time, another favourite for the locals was to deep fry a Mars bar in batter, which must have been ideal preparation for a good full on heart attack.

For most of the trip I based myself mainly around the Edinburgh area covering as many of the Type 2 diesel workings as possible, which could easily produce at least three Class 26's per day. In addition, the Edinburgh to Dundee services were still mainly in the hands of Class 27s with a number of steam heat Class 47s thrown in for good measure. The Class 26s worked most of the Edinburgh to Kirkcaldy and Fife circle services at this time and it was very interesting to watch what happened when the service arrived at Kirkcaldy. When DMU's were used there wouldn't be a problem at Kirkcaldy but a totally different issue with a locomotive and coaches. Once the service had arrived at Kirkcaldy, the train would set off to a siding alongside the mainline and once the whole train had entered the siding a second locomotive would roll up and be attached to the rear of the coaches ready to take the train back to Edinburgh. The operation was very slick and thanks to team work the train would be ready to drop back into Kirkcaldy station ready for its return to Edinburgh on time.

26011 at Kirkcaldy with the 11.35 from Edinburgh Waverley. Note the number of bashers on the platform at Kirkcaldy. 22nd August 1986.

On Friday the 22nd August 1986, I arrived in Waverley station on 26032 working the 06.47 Markinch to Edinburgh which I boarded at Inverkeithing, followed by 47117 back to Inverkeithing and a return on 26011, where I got the Gen that the 10.30 Inverness to Glasgow Queen St was booked to be worked by 37008 and 37117. A quick check of the timetable suggested I could make the train at Pitlochry by doing the 09.23 Edinburgh to Inverness, so off to Pitlochry accompanied with a bunch of Class 37 enthusiasts from South Wales. We easily made the train at Pitlochry and took it to Perth were 26028 was ready to follow the pair of 37s down to Glasgow Queen St, so quick change of plan and onto the Class 26, even though it was dud.

37008 & 37117 arrive at Pitlochry on the 10.30 Inverness to Glasgow Queen St service on the 22nd August 1986

26028 at Perth station with the 13.50 to Glasgow Queen St station on the 22nd August 1986.

The guys from South Wales informed me that the Branch Line Society (BLS), were running a charter train around Aberdeen station on Sunday the 24th August and with little else to do, I decided to head up to Aberdeen.

The day started off well with required 47201 working the 09.20 Edinburgh to Dundee, which I boarded at Inverkeithing, I must have had a lie in that day as the Dundee service was my first train of the day, pure luxury. Next it was a push pull 47 i.e., 47707 working the 09.25 Glasgow Queen St to Aberdeen, which I took north to the Granite City.

Once at Aberdeen I noticed required 37260 was working the 13.10 Aberdeen to Inverness, which I took to Dyce where I boarded the BLS special which had arrived from Aberdeen and was ready for its return to Aberdeen Waterloo Goods Yard. The special was hauled by Class 08 shunter 08882 and was soon on its way back to Aberdeen and into the yard. Once it had arrived in the yard, a number of the passengers off the special decided they wanted more excitement and either got in the cab of the shunter alongside the driver or actually hung off the shunter by its grab rails or anything else they could cling onto as it moved around in the goods yard. Another weird thing was the sudden rush of BLS members to the front vestibule of the first coach as the charter train arrived in the yard. Apparently, this enabled them to claim they had travelled as far as possible into the yard! As I said, weird!!

Need I say any more about the individuals hanging onto the Gronk!!

After the excitement of the BLS special, I headed back south to Edinburgh via Dundee and found required 27005 in position to work the 20.30 to Edinburgh, which I took all the way to Waverley for 47201 back to Inverkeithing on the 22.20 departure to Dundee.

On Monday 25th August 1986, I spent the whole day around Edinburgh and Dundee covering as many Type 2 workings as possible, before doing the overnight from Edinburgh to Inverness i.e., 23.30 Edinburgh to Inverness, to spend the morning covering the Class 37/4 which had recently taken over the services to Kyle, Wick and Thurso. This was my first time in Inverness since the 37/4s had arrived and by lunch I was heading across to Aberdeen with 47019 working the 12.25 service to Aberdeen, then down to Dundee for 47152 on the 16.30 Dundee to Edinburgh, which had its steam heat boiler in operation! I finished the day with a couple of Type 2 diesels from Edinburgh to Dunfermline with 27005 to Dunfermline for 26026 back south.

Wednesday 27th August, was the last day of my Scotty Rover, so I had to pack my bag and settle my bill, no problem with handing the key over to the Landlady, as there wasn't one. I headed to Edinburgh and spent most of the morning covering any Type 2 workings, until a massive 26003 appeared on the 11.23 Edinburgh to Perth.

26003 at Waverley station with the 11.23 to Perth. 27th August 1986.

26003 was part of a small pool of diesels classified as 26/0 which were fitted with slow speed control to enable them to work coal trains in the Fife area.

I took the Class 26 all the way to Perth for 27049 back down to Glasgow Queen Street station. Then a swift walk across to Central station to see what was heading south and my luck was certainly in as required 81003 was on the front of the 15.20 Glasgow Central to Nottingham. Unfortunately, the Class 81 had problems with its power whilst en route to Carstairs, which resulted in 30-minute delay on arrival at Carlisle, forcing them to swap the Class 81 for 47534, which certainly wasn't what I wanted but concluded a very enjoyable trip to Scotland.

To show how desperate I was to enjoy the end of Type 2 workings north of the border, I arranged another two weekend trips to Scotland on the weekends of the 19th and 20th September plus the last weekend of scheduled Type 2 diesel workings in Scotland on the weekend of 26th and 27th September 1986. For the last trip I was joined by my good friend Steve Austin, who like me, just wanted to give these distinctive engines a fond farewell. We did the usual overnight up to Glasgow from Preston station i.e., 21.00 Euston to Fort William/Inverness service. On arrival at Glasgow, we immediately headed over to Edinburgh to find a number of Class 27s working, including 27001, 27003, 27051, 27053 and 27055. Then the authorities had arranged for 27001 to work the 11.23 Edinburgh to Perth, which we took all the way and continued with 27001 down to Glasgow Queen Street on the 13.50 departure from Perth. On arrival at Queen Street, we both realised that was the end of another chapter in our railway lives. So, another swift walk across to Central station to catch the 15.20 to Nottingham and head back home. At Carstairs we were joined by Bernie Mcdonagh, who like us had made the effort to spend a day enjoying the last rites of the Class 27s, commonly known as Macrats!

27001 at Edinburgh Waverley station with the 11.23 to Perth. Thankfully, this engine made it into preservation and is now based at the Scottish Railway Preservation Society (SPRS) based at Bo'ness.

After this trip, I would only make two further trips to Scotland in pursuit of my hobby. These were October 1988 and finally during July 1993, when a group of us from the North West, were lured back north of the border with the prospect of a pair of Class 26s working a service from Inverness to Kyle of Lochalsh on Wednesdays during that summer. Thankfully on the 14th July 1993, we were once again listening to the sounds of a pair of Class 26s when 26001 and 26007 with a rake of green and white painted coaches headed off to Kyle from Inverness.

26007 & 26001 at Inverness prior to their journey to Kyle of Lochalsh.

26001 & 26007 wait to leave Kyle on their return to Inverness.

3 - Crompton Diesels

The British Railways Class 33, originally classified as B.R.C.W (Birmingham Railway Carriage & Wagon Co) Type 3, and built from 1960 to 1962 with a total of 98 built. From their introduction, the whole class was allocated to two depots on the BR Southern Region: Hither Green and Eastleigh. The class was originally split into: 86 Standards and 12 Narrow Bodied. This changed with the introduction of the push-pull version, resulting in three sub classes: 33/0, 33/1 and 33/2. The 33/0 classified as Standards and totalled 65 members, not including two members of the sub class that were withdrawn prior to them receiving their TOPS numbers. The 33/1 (aka Baggies) were equipped to work with EMU's and TC stock and were primary used on the route from Bournemouth to Weymouth following the end of steam on the Southern Region and totalled 19. Finally, 33/2 (aka Slims) were built to Hastings's line loading gauge that allowed them to pass through the narrow tunnels that exist on that line and comprised 12 locomotives.

As these were originally Southern based engines, Northern enthusiasts had little chance to see them working, unless you travelled south. I was fortunate to see them during my family holidays to Bournemouth in the mid 1960's. However, I do remember seeing D6571 haul a cement train north through Doncaster station on the 8th January 1966, this was at the time the most northerly working for the class and involved a freight service of cement tanks from Cliffe, Kent to a location in Lanarkshire, although I'm not sure if the Class 33s worked much further north than York.

With the demise of the Scottish Type 2s i.e., Class 26 and 27 which incidentally were also built by B.R.C.W, I moved my attention from north of the border to the workings of the Class 33s, which gained the nickname of 'Crompton' owing to the use of Crompton Parkinson electrical equipment on these locomotives.

During the timetable change in May 1985, British Railways had made the decision to extend the use of these locomotives to include a number of passenger services from South Wales to Manchester and Bangor in North Wales. By the 13th May 1985 one diagram involved an engine working the 07.50 Swansea to Manchester Piccadilly and 13.45 return from Manchester to Cardiff, this was a Monday to Friday diagram. On Saturdays it became the 09.02 Cardiff Central to Manchester Piccadilly with a return at 13.45 and on Sundays it involved two separate services the 15.00 Manchester Piccadilly to Cardiff Central and the 14.45 Swansea to Manchester Piccadilly service.

These services became very popular with many enthusiasts from the North West. Most week days during this period, I would pop out of the office to cover the lunch time arrival of the Swansea service from Stockport into Manchester Piccadilly.

33011 prior to working the 13.45 Manchester Piccadilly to Cardiff service on Saturday 26th October 1985.

33027 at Manchester Piccadilly with the 15.00 service to Cardiff on Sunday 27th October 1985.

My daughter Lisa aged 5 with her own notebook and pen!

By early 1986, a group of us from the North West made regular trips from Manchester down to Bristol and Bath via Newport, South Wales. At the time, there was a cheap day return ticket from Manchester to Shrewsbury plus another bargain ticket from Shrewsbury to Bristol or Cardiff. With the use of family railcards, we could get to Bristol for about £6, so this became a good way of spending those dark damp winters days. An example of one of these trips on the 22nd February 1986, we caught the 07.19 Manchester Piccadilly to Cardiff from Piccadilly to Crewe, where the electric would be changed to a Crompton i.e., 33042 on this day. This was taken through to Newport then a changed onto 33039 on the 08.10 Portsmouth to Cardiff, taken to Cardiff. Then 33037 on the 12.00 Cardiff to Crewe as far as Newport, for a Class 47 across to Bristol Temple Meads. Then it was a series of trips out and back to Bath with Crompton's including:

33016, 33117, 33056, 33033, 33117, 33050, 33030 and finally 33050 back to Cardiff for 33023 on the 18.15 Cardiff to Manchester Piccadilly as far as Crewe. The group of us included: Tom Sawyer and his son Lee, Bert Healey and his son Simon, Lenny Ball and a few others that changed from one trip to another. This carried on until one trip, when the Guard at Shrewsbury wouldn't sell us a discounted ticket to Bristol, which involved me and the guard visiting the ticket office at Shrewsbury, only to be told the offer had finished months ago and the guard who had been selling us the ticket on board the train was doing it in error. So, that was the end of our cheap days out to Cardiff and Bristol.

33056 departs Bath with the 14.10 Bristol to Portsmouth.

By May 1986, I had decided to do my first week's rover covering the services from Cardiff to Portsmouth and Basingstoke to Yeovil. I bought a Hampshire and Dorset week Rover ticket and a Wessex Rover ticket to cover as many of the Crompton hauled services as possible. Home for me during the week would be at the Railway Tavern in Salisbury, which was the start of many trips to Salisbury before the Crompton's were replaced by Class 158 DMUs. Jan and Nigel ran the pub and after about a year, they moved further down the approach road to the station to a new B&B venue, which effectively replaced the Railway Tavern.

The Railway Tavern, my home whilst staying in Salisbury.

The couples B&B establishments became very popular with railway enthusiasts and on some occasions was fully booked by them. Their new B&B venue also included a model railway layout in the breakfast area, so we could entertain ourselves whilst we waited for our cooked breakfast. It was not difficult to bump into people you knew or get to know new enthusiasts during your visits to Salisbury. One group I remember well from this time were three guys from the north and included Steve Rush and Neil Taylor, who regularly made long weekend visits to Salisbury that appeared to coincide with many of my trips. They too would always stay at the B&B places managed by Jan and Nigel.

33203 Fareham: 12.10 Cardiff to Portsmouth on the 28th May 1986.

By the timetable change in May 1988, the use of Crompton's on the Cardiff to Portsmouth, Waterloo to Yeovil routes would virtually come to an end. As a consequence, I arranged two more trips to Salisbury, the first from the 9th to the 16th April 1988 and my final trip from the 12th until 14th May 1988. Both trips would involve doing the 22.25 pm York to Shrewsbury mail service from Stalybridge to Crewe, thankfully the service had one passenger coach included in its formation. Then the 02.04 Crewe to Cardiff, which by then was booked a Class 47, at Cardiff I purchased my Rover Tickets for the week, then continued across to Bristol and finally finish at Salisbury, where I would be based for the full week. By this time the quality of the coaching stock had been allowed to deteriorate so much, that some of the stock should have been withdrawn. I presume this was all part of BR ploy to persuade it customers that when a two-coach modern DMU replaced the loco hauled trains, the customers would be impressed.

One bonus during this trip was the appearance of 33051 on the 16.15 Bristol T Meads to Weymouth, which I did throughout and 33051 return to Bristol as far as Keynsham, to end the day with 33209 on the 21.45 Bristol T Meads to Southampton from Keynsham back to Salisbury.

The final day of the trip was Saturday 16th April, coincided with an advertised Network Day and offered access to the whole of the South East network for the cost of a bargain price ticket. The majority of the day was spent between Waterloo and Exeter including a run to Exeter with 33006 and 33106 on the 08.10 Waterloo to Exeter St Davids additional service.

Last move of the day was 33112 from Grateley to Waterloo before I used the Tube to reach Euston for my train back to Manchester.

This would be my last full week of travelling behind Crompton's on the Southern, other than a short three-day trip at the end of that timetable prior to the end of the Crompton's working the Cardiff via Bristol to Portsmouth circuit.

33051 at Yeovil Pen Mill whilst working the 19.35 Weymouth to Bristol T Meads on the 11th April 1988.

4 - Cambrian Coast Summer Holiday Services

Prior to the May timetable change in 1985, Class 25s affectionately known as 'Rats', were the booked motive power to haul the summer dated services from Shrewsbury to the Cambrian coast holiday resorts. Then at the timetable change in 1985 these services were taken over by Western Region allocated Class 37s and involved three diagrams, two single Class 37s and a pair of Class 37s on the 10.55 ex Shrewsbury and 13.40 return from Aberystwyth. These services became a magnet for huge numbers of enthusiasts, especially those who followed the class, which had gained the nickname of 'Tractor' or 'Syphon'!

These summer holiday services became so popular with the enthusiasts, that most services were full and standing on leaving Shrewsbury. My first attempt to cover the new Class 37 services, was on Saturday 25th May 1985, which would have been soon after the introduction of the new summer timetable. The day started off very well with two Class 85s on hand to get me to Crewe: 85035 08.38 Manchester Pic to Newquay from Pic to Stockport, then 85024 working the 09.00 Manchester Pic to Plymouth, which took me to Crewe. Then it was 47454 from Crewe to Shrewsbury whilst working the 07.05 Holyhead to Cardiff. Arrival at Shrewsbury found Class Forty 40013 on display as an exhibition train.

40013 on display at Shrewsbury on the 25th May 1985

The festivities started with the arrival of the 07.30 Euston to Aberystwyth with 47532 hauling the train on arrival at Shrewsbury. This was detached and 37023 and 37066 rolled up to the rear and were hooked up ready for the journey to Aberystwyth. The planned move involved the pair to Caersws for the single Class 37 (37126) on the 11.00 Aberystwyth to Euston back to Welshpool, then another single Class 37 (37142) on the 09.35 Euston to Aberystwyth from Welshpool back to Caersws. As the returning pair from Aberystwyth didn't arrive for over an hour, several hundred bashers descended on this small mid Wales village, which offered a couple of Pubs and a chippy. The Chippy owner must have thought that Christmas had come early, with a huge queue of eager customers keen to get their lunch before the pair of Class 37s returned. There must be many a tale told about these stop overs at Caersws but the two most noteworthy must include the day when a fairly infamous TTI followed the bashers into Caersws and started to check people's tickets to ensure they had a legitimate ticket, don't know how that would have gone down if it had gone to court? The other occasion was when a number of fairly common Class 37s had been allocated to work the Cambrian Coast, resulting in very few bashers making the effort to cover them. This certainly caused the Chippy owner major problems as he had already prepared tons of Chips ready for the invasion of bashers, only to find little more than a dozen enthusiasts turn up at his Chippy.

After enjoying the pleasures of Caersws, it was time to head back to the station to catch the pair on the 13.40 Aberystwyth to Shrewsbury, which was regularly extended to Wolverhampton during that summer. The station platform at Caersws was full to over flowing with bashers who were either full of fish and chips or beer. The pair arrived on time and off to Shrewsbury we went. At Shrewsbury rumours started to circulate that the train would be extended to Wolverhampton and sure enough a pair of Class 25s, backed onto the stock. 25195 and 25313, did the honours and thoroughly entertained us on the journey to Wolverhampton. This was very appropriate, as the Class 25s had only just been replaced by the Class 37s on the Cambrian Coast summer services.

25230 & 25191 at Wolverhampton with the 16.20 Shrewsbury to Wolves relief on the 22nd June 1985

Unfortunately, many of us will remember that the Cambrian Coast also attracted a number of undesirables who were either off their heads or just simply mad. On one occasion whilst waiting for the second Euston to Aberystwyth service to arrive, a bunch of so-called enthusiasts left the station and got into a works yard alongside the station. They somehow managed to start up a tractor unit similar to a JCB and then drove it in circles around the yard smashing into loads of equipment. How on earth one of the idiots didn't get injured is beyond me. Another even worse example, was on one of the trains I was looking out of the window of one of the coaches and watched one of these nutters dragged himself out of the door window by grabbing hold of the roof guttering and then standing on the window with his entire body hanging on the outside of the train. Unfortunately, I'm not making this up, it actually happened and just begs the question, what was going on in his head at the time! The problems became so bad that the train started to be patrolled by British Transport Police in an attempt to stop a few mindless idiots from ruining a very sociable day in Mid Wales.

Gone are those days and I wouldn't be surprised if these services on a Summer Saturday are now just a few DMUs with the bulk of the holidaymakers making their own arrangements to travel to these coastal resorts.

37070 at Welshpool on the 13th June 1987 whilst working the 07.40 Euston to Pwllheli.

5 - Summer Services in the 1980s

As mentioned earlier, the busiest time of year for bashing was the weekends in the summer, when huge numbers of additional trains operated across the network to deliver thousands of families to the holiday resorts. This was good business for the railways and often stretched their resources to the limit and forced the management to use locomotives that would usually be hauling freight trains. This gave the basher the opportunity to fill those voids in their books. For example: Immingham Class 47s would usually be employed on hauling heavy freights or those huge numbers of Class 20s that were, for most of the year kept busy ferrying coal from the Pits to Power Stations.

I first took advantage of these workings in the late 1970s and early 1980s when each August Bank Holiday I would buy an East Midlands Rover ticket that allowed unlimited travel within a specified area of the East Midlands for up to a week. The route from Derby to Sheffield was heavily used by cross country services and during the summer, to ease the loadings on scheduled services, would result in many relief services operating. These included many services that started in South Wales or Bristol and travelled north to Leeds, York or Newcastle. In addition, reliefs were run to Scarborough, Skegness and Yarmouth that could easily be covered by the Rover Ticket.

37169 arriving at Rotherham with the 08.55 Sheffield to Cleethorpes on the 31st August 1983.

46028 departs Sheffield with the 08.20 Leeds to Weymouth on the 31st August 1983

The first important thing to do after arrival at Sheffield was to try and get the gen on what was working the various reliefs that day. Usually, one of the locals would have a complete list of which reliefs were running and what was hauling them. You then adjusted your days plans around the best possible way to cover those reliefs that you required and did your best to avoid the likes of: Class 31/4, 45/1 or 47/4. Sometimes the planners must have really struggled to get the motive power to haul the booked relief trains. This was definitely the case on the 25th August 1985, when York was forced to use a single Class 20: 20011 on the 12.55 York to Birmingham relief.

20011 on its own departing Derby with the 12.55 York to Birmingham New Street Relief 25th August 1985

During the course of the week, I would frequently, head over to Skegness by mid-afternoon to see what was ready to depart the resort later in the day. Most days at least four trains would be scheduled to leave but during Bank holiday times this could number 6 or 7, bolstered by a number of reliefs. The bulk of these trains would be hauled by a pair of

Class 20s that had destinations including Nottingham, Leicester and Derby. In addition to the Class 20s, members of Class 31s, 37s and 47s were frequently used.

20085 and 20059 at the buffer stops at Skegness on the 27th August 1990 after arriving from Derby.

Another benefit of the ticket was there was an opportunity to have a Tinsley based Class 08 Gronk during the afternoon when two trains from Leeds and Hull were joined together. This involved the Gronk shunting the Hull portion including the passengers on board across to the rear of the portion from Leeds. After this manoeuvre the whole train would continue onto Brighton. One of the regular Gronks was 08878, which I managed to have on the 23rd July 1985. Unfortunately, the platform staff at Sheffield tried their best to stop anyone from boarding the train and this could involve them dragging individuals off the train who had managed to sneak past them. To be honest, they were completely out of order and only did it to annoy the enthusiasts. I suspect this was their way of trying to prove to enthusiasts they had the power and means to do whatever they wanted. However, I'm sure if the authorities had taken an individual to court the case would have been thrown out as being inappropriate, especially, when the portion was often sat in the platform for up to 5 minutes and other passengers just got off and re-joined the train as they pleased.

Another weird thing that happened was at Chesterfield station, where the station staff created a fenced off area on the south bound platform. This pen was supposed to be there for the benefit of train spotters and to stop these individuals from being on the platform. In addition, the ticket staff at Chesterfield tried their best to stop the rail enthusiast from changing platforms by carrying out ticket checks on all those who decided to change from the south bound to the north bound platform. Needless to say, they didn't do a very good job and just ended up annoying not only the rail enthusiasts but many members of the public who were trying to exit the station but were forced to queue whilst the checks were completed.

During this period, it was also possible to get some fairly unusual haulage other than freight locomotives. One good example was when a Class 50 locomotives became due a visit to Doncaster works for overhaul, the Western Region would arrange for the locomotive in question to work a passenger service north, for example: 09.18 Penzance to

Leeds and on the 27th August 1985, I witnessed this happen when 50009 worked the train as far as Sheffield where it was removed prior to its journey to Doncaster.

50009 at Sheffield after arriving with the 09.18 Penzance to Leeds.

20146 & 20176 reverse their train to the carriage sidings at Derby after arriving with a service from Skegness on 24th August 1985.

6 – Railtours and Special Events

With this surge in interest in the railways a number of companies sprang up whose sole purpose was to provide special trains for the rail enthusiast market. Two of the most popular companies at the time included: Pathfinder and Hertfordshire Railtours. They quickly realised that if they provided the right motive power and travelled along an interesting route, they could make good money from running these trains. There were many more companies but the two mentioned were basically the main players in the market.

As the railways became more sectorised it started to be more difficult to find freight locomotives on passenger services which became more apparent by the late 1980s. By which time, there had been a significant drop in freight engines being used on passenger services, including the summer holiday traffic.

Consequently, a group of us from the North West would regularly book on any railtour or Special event that included locomotives that were considered interesting enough to travel the length of the country. This included the series of specials run over the Settle and Carlisle line during November 1989 which were usually organised by Maurice Broadhead. I first met Maurice back in September 1985 when we both did the overnight up from Edinburgh to

Inverness. Maurice organised a series of specials to run from Leeds to Carlisle on each Saturday during November 1989. The first on the 4th November involved 56104 with 47503 supplying the heat for the train, next came 56030 with 47475 supplying the heat on the 11th November, next it was the turn of 56099 with 47477 supplying the heat. Then finally the Piece de resistance when 20061 with 20093 and 47444 were used on the 08.25 Leeds to Carlisle and return from Carlisle at 12.42.

20061, 20093 and 47444 prior to departure from Carlisle Citadel station on the 25th November 1989.

Maurice didn't let the grass grow under his feet, as by the 24th February 1990, he was running a further series of specials along the Settle and Carlisle line, starting on the 24th February 1990 with two return specials one with Class 25

D7672 and 47422 working the 08.22 Leeds to Carlisle and return and a second service with 26007 and 47443 working the 06.34 Carlisle to Leeds and return from Leeds at 10.45. Journeys behind both sets of engines could easily be worked out and in my case involved a quick return trip up to Keighley followed by a return trip to Appleby.

Then on the 10th March 1990, he organised a further trip again with two train sets, including 37104 and 47456 on the 08.25 Leeds to Carlisle and return, plus outrageous 20905, 20906 and 47422 on the second train which did the 06.34 Carlisle to Leeds and 10.45 return from Leeds. The service with the Class 20's proved so popular that it was estimated that well over a thousand customers travelled on it that day.

The final Settle and Carlisle special happened on the 17th March 1990 when 56075 with 47453 supplying train heat only, worked the 08.25 Leeds to Carlisle and 12.42 return from Carlisle. Surprisingly, on arrival at Carlisle we found 31200 ready to work the 11.35 to Newcastle, so this was done to the first shack at Wetheral for a DMU back to Carlisle in time for the return with 56075. In those days the North Pennine services were still in the hands of Class 47/4s, so the day finished with a return from Leeds to Stalybridge with 47597 hauling the 14.22 Newcastle to Liverpool Lime Street. In theory, we could have had the Class 47 all the way from Newcastle if we had stayed on 31200 from Carlisle to Newcastle but that would have been a bad move!

The impressive sight of 20906 & 20905 at Leeds before departing with the 10.45 to Carlisle, 10th March 1990

31200 at Carlisle with the 11.35 to Newcastle.

The railtours started to come thick and fast and the next notable working was the 'Vladivostok Avoider' run by the Class 20 Locomotive Society on the 12th May 1990. Thanks to Steve Kemp, we found out that the engines would work the ECS (Empty Coaching Stock) movement from Stockport Edgeley carriage sidings to Sheffield and return. So, after a few 'phone calls we managed to board the stock at Stockport with 20132 and 20010 at the business end. This was taken across to Sheffield where the special started its circular route of Yorkshire, calling at Scarborough then south via Filey and the Hull avoider for the return to Sheffield. Here, we were once again allowed to stay on the stock as long as we helped to clear up the rubbish, so thirty full black bin bags later we were done and dusted.

20010 & 20132 at Bridlington during a 30-minute scheduled stop, so customers could stretch their legs.

Virtually every weekend, we were booked on a railtour with just too many to list or mention. The next memorable railtour happened on the 13th April 1991, when the 'Solent Growler' was run by the Growler Group. The tour started at Manchester Piccadilly and was booked to head south and involved a visit to Southampton East Docks with a pair of Tractors. On the day we boarded the train at Stockport at an unearthly hour of 05.32, suspect this involved parking the car at Stockport for the day. Our group comprised of myself, Pete Yarwood and Mark Love, who very conveniently lived a short walk from Edgeley station. Thankfully, we were located in the front coach along with many other friends who fully appreciated the full sound of 37272 and 37032 for the entire journey as the stock didn't change direction. A number of problems occurred at Southampton but nothing too big and resulted in an unscheduled stop at Didcot.

37272 & 37032 entering Southampton East Dock

The trip became memorable because the three of us got completely wasted, as a result of drinking beer on the way south then finishing off a bottle of whiskey that one of us won in the raffle. Then finally after a visit to a pub during our stop at Didcot, we were completely finished, I suspect my own children would have been embarrassed with our antics that day but who gives a damn as we all enjoyed the day immensely.

37272 & 37032 rest at Didcot with friend Tom Sawyer keeping an eye on proceedings.

It's impossible to list all the specials we did at this time as most weekends we were out and about at some sort of event or gala. However, I must mention our involvement on the Pathfinder 'Coal Scuttler' Railtour run over the weekend of the 24th and 26th May 1991. This was the first time I'd ever been on a railtour that involved an overnight. The railtour started at Bristol at 06.12 and we boarded the train at Warrington Bank Quay station where 20131 and 20175 replaced the Duff that had started the tour off from Bristol, so nothing lost there then. For once our party was located in the rear coach, which was unusual as we usually booked between a half and a full coach to accommodate our group. The only benefit of this would be that we would be in the front coach for the trips down the branch lines the tour was scheduled to visit. The Class 20s took us up to Carlisle where they were replaced by 37245 and 26038 for the journey across to Falkland Yard near Ayr. Then we visited two former Colliery branches in Ayrshire at: Killoch and Waterside, with 20138 and 20124 plus 26002 and 26007 working top and tail to visit each branch before heading back to Ayr for a well-earned four-hour break. With the knowledge that we would be in Ayr for so long, we prebooked a table at a real ale pub that served fabulous food. Around a dozen of us took full advantage of the pub's hospitality, whilst some of the other railtour customers gathered outside our window to watch us enjoy the home cooked food along with plenty of beer. To be honest it was the best bit of planning we had ever done and fully relaxed us prior to our overnight journey to the Open Day at Coalville.

After thoroughly enjoying our visit to the pub, it was time for the return south with 37245 and 26038 once again hauling the railtour back to Carlisle then 20013 and 20141 down to Preston. Where, 56018 took us across to Derby including a quick visit to the Denby branch then 56015 over to the Open Day at Coalville where they used 58048 to shunt release our train. Then it was the turn of 60057 and 60032 from Coalville to Nuneaton for finally 56021 back to Birmingham New Street, where we got off the tour and headed back home. To be honest, a truly memorable railtour and worth every penny.

26038 with 37245 hidden behind the Class 20's: 20131 and 20175 during the engine change at Carlisle Citadel station during the running of the 'Coal Scuttle' Railtour.

I stopped doing UK railtours during the mid-1990's when the EWS Class 66 (aka Sheds) diesels became a regular feature of most railtours. At the same time my interest in travelling abroad just took off!

7 – Portugal

By 1994 I dipped my toe into the world of foreign railways for the first time, or as some of my railway friends would say, foreign muck!! Following my divorce in the early 1990s, I met June who lived close by and we eventually became partners, which involved enjoying holidays together. At first, we went to places in England but a work colleague of June's owned a Villa in Albuferia, Portugal, who kindly offered it to us for a week. So, after booking flights we were all ready for our first foreign holiday as a couple. We flew out from Manchester to Faro in Sunday 30th October 1994 with a charter airline called Ambassador, which was declared bankrupt by the 28th November 1994. Too close for comfort!

Ambassador Airlines Airbus A300-200: SX-BSJ

Their Airbus A300-200 series SX-BSJ arrived late at Faro as there were issues before we departed Manchester, I suspect they needed to pay a few bills before they were allowed to take off. We, eventually landed four hours late, by which time it was dark, which didn't help as I had hired a car to take us from Faro Airport to our Villa. Somehow, we managed to leave the airport safely and amazingly found our Villa in Albuferia. The Villa was well-furnished and conveniently close to a number of bars and restaurants, which we took full advantage of during our holiday.

Our Villa in Albuferia with June posing outside.

We spent the first full day getting to know our new holiday resort, which was well before it became a popular holiday destination. Albuferia was a great location with an unspoilt beach and plenty of bar/restaurants to enjoy.

Prior to going on holiday, I had spoken to a number of friends who had been to Portugal purely from a railway perspective, to try and understand how the railways worked on the Algarve.

By the second day we decided to spend a day in Lagos, which is located at the south west tip of Portugal and had a train service from the nearby town of Tunes. By mid-morning, we drove across to Tunes and dumped the car at the station, then purchased our return tickets to Lagos.

Left: Our tickets to Lagos   Right: The CP Timetable for 1995/96

If I remember correctly, there used to be about 240 Escudo to the £ at the time of our visit, so the trip to Lagos would have cost less than £6 for the two of us. After taking a few photographs at Tunes, we heading west behind French built

Class 1200: 1211 working the 08.55 Vila Real de St Antonio Guadiana to Lagos. The service arrived with Alco 1503 piloting 1211 into Tunes but unfortunately the Alco was removed at Tunes. The CP 1200 got the nickname of 'Sewing Machines', owing to their total lack of power and thrash!

CP 1211 after arrival at Lagos at 13.00 on the 1st November 1994.

We spent most of the afternoon walking around this beautiful Portuguese coastal town before it was time to head back to the station for the 17.00 Lagos to Tunes, which was a portion to Barreiro south of Lisboa. I had already been told that this service was booked a Class 1400. The first ten of class were originally built at the English Electric Vulcan Foundry at Newton-Le-Willows, England, then the remainder were built under licence in Portugal.

Needless to say, the CP 1400 made an impressive racket, which was even more evident when you sat immediately behind the engine with the windows fully open on the return journey. The line here is relatively flat and crosses a number of bridges over estuaries from the nearby coastline.

CP 1455 at Lagos with the 17.00 to Tunes and portion to Barreiro.

On return to Tunes, I managed to see my first CP 1800, with the arrival of 1805 working the 16.15 Vila Real De St Antonio Guadiana to Barreiro Inter Regional Service. The CP 1800 were a development of the English Electric Class 50, with a lot of the sophisticated electrical equipment simplified. All ten were built at the Vulcan Foundry but to the wider Iberian gauge, just marginally larger the 5ft 5 inches.

CP 1805 at Tunes with the Barreiro service 1st Nov 1994.

Tunes was the junction on the Algarve where the line from the Spanish border at Vila Real de Antonio Guadiana split to Lagos and north to Barreiro on the opposite side of the River Tagus from Lisboa. Tunes could be a fairly quiet place at the best of times but at the time of 1805 arrival the station had two services to Lagos plus a freight in the station yard.

The following day I had convinced June that a trip to Tavira would be a good idea. Tavira is a beautiful fishing village further along the coast on the Algarve and provided the opportunity for some more haulage. After a quick look at the CP Timetable whilst at Tunes, I decide to aim for the morning Inter Regional from Barreiro but this time from Albuferia. We drove from the Villa to Albuferia station, which had a convenient bar, so coffees were enjoyed before our train arrived. The Inter Regional services to the Algarve were booked CP 1800s, so I was truly surprised when a 1948 built Class 1501 arrived with the 08.35 from Barreiro. These American built switcher diesels were Portugal's first diesel locomotives and 1501 was actually four years older than me.

CP 1501 arriving at Albuferia station with the 08.35 from Barreiro.

Even more surprising was when the train arrived at Loule whilst en route to Faro, we were joined by a bunch of British Bashers who I knew from my days back in the UK. This really wound June up, who was suspicious that this had all been pre-planned. The guys were part way through a weeklong visit to Portugal and had come down on the overnight from Barreiro to spend some time on the Algarve. They immediately started to reel off the engines they had seen in the north around Porto and Entroncamento. I suspect it was this encounter that fired up my interest in the railways in Portugal and eventually all over Europe.

1501 after arrival at Tavira.

After the trip to Tavira, we would either use the railway to visit places of interest or I would find time for a quick visit to Tunes to take some phots or even a short return trip. Portugal had ignited the blue touch paper and would be the start of many more trips to mainland Europe and beyond.

On Saturday the 5th November, our last full day in Portugal, we decided to visit the Spanish border at Vila Real de St Antonio Guadiana. We drove to Albuferia and boarded the 09.33 Lagos to Faro with a pair of Class 1200s: 1221 and 1223 which we took to Faro for a short break before joining the 08.35 from Barreiro which this time was hauled by 1810.

Left: 1223 and 1221 at Faro.
Right: 1810 at Faro prior to our journey towards the Spanish Border.

I remember enjoying the journey behind 1810 and managed to find a couple of seats not far from the engine. Soon after 14.00 pm we were arriving at our destination, followed by a walk down to the river to see if we could catch a boat across the river Guadiana to Spain. Unfortunately, when we arrived in the Spanish town of Ayamonte, they were well into their afternoon Siesta, so the place was virtually shut! A quick about turn and back on the boat to Portugal. Here we enjoyed some Portuguese hospitality and finally departed on the 19.05 Vila Real de St Antonio Guadiana to Tunes as far as Albuferia with 1207 hauling the train.

The following day we flew back to Manchester on a Monarch Airlines A300-600: G-OJMR - photo on the next page. This was the first wide bodied jet I'd ever flown on and with my back ground in aeronautical engineering, I was suitably impressed with the incredible size of the fuselage.

Back home, I started to plan my next European trip with the first being a day trip to the Irish Republic, more about that in the next chapter.

After purchasing a CP Timetable, I started to plan my first week long trip to Portugal, which would start on the 25th March 1995. By then, Caledonian Airlines had started a scheduled service from Manchester to Faro, so flights sorted. At that time, this was done via a Travel Agency, no on-line booking systems back then or in fact no Internet was readily available.

Following numerous 'phone calls, I found out that CP offered a week All Line First Class Rover ticket for 17,000 Escudo, which roughly worked out at £70, so fantastic value. The ticket was known as the 'Bilhete Turistico' and could be purchased from most large stations, including Faro. The next problem, was where to stay during my tour of the country, again a few suggestions were made and thankfully these came in very useful.

Above: My 'Bilhete Turistico' ticket, dated 25th March 1995.

My flights were booked to depart on the Saturday 25th March and return on Saturday 1st April 1995. The departure was nice and early at 07.00 am and took just over two and half hours to reach Faro, in a Lockheed Tri-Star G-BBAH. This was my first Tri-Star I had flown on and was truly impressed and managed to get a window seat for the flight south.

On arrival at Faro airport, I had been told to take a taxi to the station, as taxis were relatively cheap in Faro. Of course, the taxi driver wanted to take me further, especially when he found I planned to head north to Lisboa. He must have thought Christmas had come early, sorry mate but its Faro station only! At the station I soon obtained my CP Rover ticket after acquiring some local currency. Back then, I doubt that the ticket office at Faro could handle credit cards payments, so it was cash only. The weather was fabulous and I was soon regretting bringing a thick coat. By 12.20 pm I was on my first move of the trip and took 1218 on the 12.20 Faro to Lagos as far as Loule to catch the morning

Inter Regional 08.35 from Barreiro with dud 1806 back to Faro. Not impressed, but then it was time for my first Class 1931, a French Alsthom design, which the Portuguese had decided to remove the silencers on their engines. This made these diesels about the loudest diesel I had ever heard and were very impressive. Unfortunately, the Rapido Services which they worked, used fully air-conditioned coaches, which reduced the sound effects of these monsters.

The 14.15 Faro to Barreiro had 1937 hooked on the front and required a reservation for a seat, so this was acquired for a seat in the front coach for the trip from Faro to Tunes. Even with the sealed windows the noise of the exhaust, sounded just like hundreds of machine guns going off simultaneously.

CP 1937 with the 1415 Faro to Barreiro Rapido Service.

After arrival at Tunes, I covered a few Sewing Machines that worked the stopping services along the Algarve coast, then off to Silves to pick up the 17.00 Lagos to Tunes, which was booked to be hauled by a CP 1400. Bang on time 1442 turned up and was taken back to Tunes.

CP 1442 after arrival at Tunes with the 17.00 from Lagos.

I spent the rest of the afternoon covering various trains including 1944 working the 18.15 Rapido from Barreiro which I took back to Faro. I had time for an evening meal, so found a convenient restaurant and enjoyed a great meal with my first Portuguese beer of the trip, several bottles of Sagres, which is a light beer and very enjoyable.

The plan was to do the overnight service off Faro, all the way to Barreiro, which was booked to depart Faro at 23.00. The 21.40 Vila Real de St Antonio Guadiana to Barreiro was scheduled to stop in Faro for five minutes before its departure north. So, I took no chances and was stood on the platform at Faro by 22.45 and to my surprise I was joined by three Yorkshire lads including Nigel Pearson aka Harrogate and Woodlesford, sorry I just can't remember the name of the third person, put it down to an age thing!

To be honest, I was fortunate to have company as this would be the first time, I had ever travelled on an overnight train service abroad and didn't know what to expect. A few years later a friend of mine had his bag stolen whilst doing the exact same train, so having company was a much safer way to travel. The coach we boarded was all compartments and it didn't take long before we found two that were empty. The seats were the long bench style and perfect to crash out on for our 6-hour 40-minute journey north.

I had worked out a plan to cover numerous local services on our arrival at Barreiro but this was thrown into chaos as I had forgotten the clocks went forward by an hour that night. So, we actually arrived at 06.40 as opposed to 05.40. However, we must have been early as I managed to board the 06.25 service to Setubal with Alco 1512. Took this all the way to Setubal for another Alco 1502 on the 07.25 from Setubal, another two Alco's were slotted into the book 1505 and 1521 before it was time to relax on a ferry across the river Tagus.

At the time, the Ferry service was also operated by Portuguese railways. So, in theory my ticket should have been sufficient but usually the guys on the barrier insisted the ticket wasn't valid and you were forced to spend a few extra Escudo for the trip across to Lisboa. My ferry that day was named 'Estremadura' and was the 09.45 departure from Barreiro to the ferry terminal at Lisboa.

Left: CP 1512 at Barreiro with the 06.25 to Setubal.
Right: One of the CP Ferries arriving at the ferry terminal at Barreiro.

I decided to sit on the top deck as the weather was incredibly pleasant and provided time for a very relaxed crossing of the river. I had a plan which involved covering some old electric and diesel diagrams off Entroncamento, which would hopefully involve my first night in an hotel. So, I did a CP Class 2600 electric 2611 on the IC Rapido at 11.00 to Porto up to Entroncamento. This gave me 15 minutes or so, to do some photography and time to visit the station bar and purchase my first Portuguese egg tart cakes for lunch. The Portuguese just love their cakes and most station bars had a vast array of cakes on display. This would usually be enjoyed with a large glass of Galão, an expresso coffee with foamed milk, simply delicious. More about the food and drink in Portugal later.

Next, it was time to enjoy some vintage electric power in the shape of CP Class 2501: 2513 working the 07.50 Covillã to Lisboa Santa Apolonia (SA). These electrics were first introduced back in 1956-57 and were the first of two batches of main line electric locomotive built by or under licence from Alsthom-Henschel before the French built Class 2600 arrived. After arriving back at Entrocamento, it was time to check into the Hotel Gameiro located across from the station, which had been recommended to me. My first problem was that the receptionist spoke very little English, even less than my Portuguese! Thankfully, I eventually managed to book a room for one night but can't remember if this included breakfast but the bedroom was clean and comfortable and most importantly was en-suite!

Left: 2611 11.00 IC Rapido service to Porto at Lisboa SA station.
Right: CP old electric 2513 at Santarem station.

After eventually sorting out my room at the hotel and dumping the bulk of the contents of my bag in the room, it was straight back to station for a series of diesel moves including my first CP 1551: 1570 on the 12.30 Lisboa SA to Covillã, which I took up to Ródão for a longish wait for the Sunday only 17.20 Ródão to Lisboa SA. Whilst at Ródão, I viewed 1933 on the 15.15 Covillã to Lisboa SA, which didn't stop at Ródão. Eventually, 1450 (Coimbra B allocated) appeared with the ecs that formed the 17.20 departure.

Left: CP 1570 at Ródão with the 12.30 from Lisboa SA.
Right: 1450 arrives at Ródão, prior to working the 17.20 to Lisboa SA.

I got off 1450 at a shack called Alvegã Ortiga, so I could cover two more CP 1551 diagrams: 1561 working the 15.23 Covillã to Lisboa SA which I did to a shack past Abrantes called Tramagal then 1553 working the 17.09 Lisboa SA to Covillã back to Abrantes. Abrantes was where the overhead wires started for services to Entroncamento and beyond, so most long-distance services had an engine change here. However, services along Table 120 to Elvas and Badajoz on the Spanish border usually had a diesel throughout from Entroncamento to their destination, which on this day included 1436 working the 18.50 Entroncamento to Elvas, which I took to Ponte de Sor. Then it was the turn of 1444 on the 17.50 Badajoz to Entroncamento through to its destination. The end of a very enjoyable day which went unbelievably well considering this was my first visit.
At the hotel it was time for a well-earned shower and freshen up after 2 days on the move. Unfortunately, the local dogs did their best to keep me awake but thankfully sleep won the day.

Left: CP 1561 at Tramagal   Right: 1444 arrives at Ponte De Sor.

The next day I planned to cover one of the few hauled services that went to the terminus station at Coimbra as opposed to Coimbra B. This involved catching the 07.22 Lisboa SA to Guarda with 2628 to Coimbra B. Then waited for 1440 and 1460 to arrive with the 05.30 from Mangualde.

Coimbra is a university city with a vast amount of history and to be honest I should have spent longer there but the urge to bash soon took over. So, I took an EMU back to Coimbra B and waited for old electric 2569 to arrive with the 08.10 Lisboa SA to Guarda, which was taken through to Pampilhosa, where an engine change was required as the line to the Spanish border was not electrified at this time.

Left: Then 2569 at Pampilhosa, prior to being replaced by 1967.
Right: 1440 and 1460 after arrival at Coimbra station.

71

Here Class 1961: 1967 dropped onto the train, which I took forward to Luso Bacaco for a very tight connection onto 1565 whilst working the 08.20 Guarda to Coimbra. The CP 1961s are a relatively small class of thirteen engines built by Bombardier in Montreal, Canada and by then had gained the nickname of 'Dumper Truck', owing to the strange appearance. Table 110 was at the time the only place that 1961s had any diagrams to work passenger services and with the line scheduled to be electrified in the near future, chasing 1961s became a priority. It wasn't helped by the fact that they only had a handful of passenger diagrams.

Back at Coimbra B, I again headed north with 2622 on the 12.30 Lisboa SA to Guarda back to Pampilhosa where 1964 dropped onto the train which was taken forward to Santa Comba Dao. Then it was a series of services back down to Lisboa SA prior to my overnight up to Porto Campanha.

Left: 1964 at Santa Comba with the 12.30 from Lisboa SA.
Right: 2503 backs onto the 15.25 Guarda to Lisboa SA at Pampilhosa.

My wait at Lisboa SA was considerably shorter than originally planned as the 20.10 Castelo Branco to Lisboa SA was running about 33 minutes late. It was originally scheduled to arrive in Lisboa SA at 23.25 then onto my overnight which was scheduled to departed at 00.20. In the end I had about 10 minutes to board my overnight and thankfully found an empty compartment to crash out in. 2609 was provided for the overnight up to Porto, where the train arrived before 07.00 am, allowing me all morning to cover the Porto Class 1400s working the commuter services in and out of Porto. During the day I must have picked up at least a dozen 1400s including a Gronk move behind CP Class 1151: 1180. The 1151s are a Rolls Royce powered sentinel diesel and frequently used to release 1400s from the buffer stops at the terminus station of Porto Sao Bento. These diminutive engines would draw the coaches into the tunnel at the entrance to the station, enabling the 1400 to drop onto the front of another set of coaches.

1180 Port Sao Bento plus some of the Art work at Sao Bento station.

Porto Sao Bento station is a real architectural gem with impressive historic tiled scenes on the walls of the main foyer of the station. The trip to Porto was aimed at getting as many 1400s as possible before heading south again. Future trips would usually involve an overnight stay in this northern city. By 20.15 pm, I was again heading back south to stay at the Hotel Gameiro at Entroncamento, which I had manage to prebook during my earlier visit. On arrival at Entroncamento, I viewed 1567 arrive with the 20.10 Castelo Branco to Lisboa SA then it was off to the hotel for some well-earned doss. This time I had booked to stay for 2 nights at the hotel and used it as a base to cover some old electric and Alco Class 1551s.

Entroncamento, was a fairly sociable place to stay and provided a number of bars and restaurants on the road that overlooked the railway line. One of these bars had a huge hot grill in the middle of the bar area, where staff would knock up grilled pork chops etc which was washed down with plenty of Sagres beer. They also kept you supplied with plenty of snacks to help your appetite for more beer.

The following day Wednesday 29th March, I was on the station in time to watch 1432 arrive with the 05.10 from Elvas before taking 1457 on the 09.10 Entroncamento to Badajoz to Santo Margarida then 1570 back to Abrantes on the 08.10 Lisboa SA to Castelo Branco. After a fester at Abrantes, 1556 eventually turned up with the 07.50 Covillã to Lisboa SA, which I did to Entroncamento for old electric 2552 (old body style) which worked the train forward to Lisboa SA. I took this to Santarem for 2606 back to Entroncamento on the 12.30 Lisboa SA to Guarda. Next obvious move from Entroncamento involved a huge fester at Abrantes but the decision was made for me when required 1567 dropped onto the portion off the 12.30 from Lisboa SA for Covillã and departed Entroncamento at 14.14 pm, it was scheduled to depart Abrantes at 13.45 which would normally allow you time to go through to Castelo Branco on the Alco and easily make the 15.15 Rapido IC from Covillã to Lisboa SA. However, the north bound was retimed and would almost certainly miss the Rapido IC at Castelo Branco. So basically, my only option was a massive long wait at Abrantes with absolutely nothing else to do. After visiting a shop close to the station about ten times, I had the pleasure of watching 1555 arrive with a very short freight, it then began to carryout various shunting manoeuvres at Abrantes.

Left: 1555 at Abrantes.   Right: 1332 & 1327 at Entroncamento.

Then dud 1941 turned up on the Rapido IC and departed at 17.39, which I took back to Entroncamento. Here, 1460 was on the 18.50 to Elvas, which departed 19.03 and was taken through to Ponte De Sor for 1444 on the 17.50 Badajoz to

Entroncamento. Then off to a bar for beers and food before retiring for the night.

The next day it was time to start my journey back south with the afternoon spent around Barreiro. I took 2604 on the 03.35 Covillã to Lisboa SA at 07.55 through to Lisboa SA then walked to the Ferry terminal for my trip across to Barreiro, I couldn't believe that CP had provided the same boat as the one used to cross the river at the start of the trip i.e., Estremadura. My first move off Barreiro was with 1465 working the 10.35 to Praias Sado which I took to Pinhal Novo after which I did numerous commuter services until my overnight was scheduled to leave at 23.50. By mid-afternoon I had bumped into the Yorkshire guys again and included a visit to a local bar near Pinhal Novo station where we enjoyed a superb Chicken meal and the odd beer before heading back to the station to cover the 20.28 Barreiro to Setubal, which was booked to be worked by a Class 1931 on stock with full drop-down windows. We located ourselves in the front coach and dropped all the windows down to enjoy the full audio effects of this unsilenced monster. Then two of the Yorkshire guys decided to start Aeroplaning whilst standing on the steps of the open front doors of the coach whilst holding onto the hand rails. Needless to say, this completely blow up the Guard who just couldn't understand what they were doing. The noise of the 1944 was completely outrageous and must have gone down very badly with any locals who lived close to the line to Setubal. After arrival at Setubal required Alco 1525 arrived with the

16.15 Vila Real de St Antonia Guadiana to Barreiro then 1521 on the 22.20 Setubal to Barreiro from Pinhal Novo back to Barreiro.

CP 1944 after arrival at Setubal.   CP Ferry crossing the Tagus.

Then finally it was the turn of 1807 on the 23.50 Barreiro to Vila Real de St Antonio **Guadiana** all the way to Tunes. I seem to recall having a compartment all to myself on the journey south with the window slightly open to experience the full stereophonic sound of the Class 1800 up front.

For those not familiar with the CP 1800s, they are basically a development of the British Rail Class 50 but with many of the complicated electronics removed. Because of their heritage they gained a huge following from the UK and it was not unusual to bump into someone from the UK whilst on a trip to Portugal.

After arriving at Tunes, I continued to Lagos on the rear portion of the train that I had arrived on from Barreiro. This became the 05.25 Tunes to Lagos with required Sawing Machine 1220 and delivered me to Lagos in plenty of time to catch the 06.55 Lagos to Tunes, booked a Class 1400:

1442. I took this back to Tunes and spent the last full day of the trip along the Algarve coast before finishing the day in Faro and finding a convenient hotel to spend my last night.

Saturday 1st April 1995, was the last day of a very enjoyable first adventure abroad dedicated purely to bashing engines. As my flight wasn't until 13.05, I opted to do a simple out and back from Faro to Tavira, which allowed me to cover the inbound 1800 from Vila Real St Antonio **Guadiana**.

Unfortunately, this involved an DMU from Faro to Tavira, where I boarded the train with 1803 up front. The 1800 would only work as far as Faro, where it would be refuelled and made ready for its return north later in the day.

CP 1803 at Tavira on my last day.   The Caledonian Tri-Star at Faro.

Back at Faro, I caught a taxi to airport, which brought down the curtain on an excellent trip. Then back to Manchester on the same Caledonian Tri-Star that I had on the flight from Manchester a week earlier.

My next trip happened during April 1996, when myself and two friends: Mark Ward and Haydn Pollitt booked a week in sunny Portugal. The dates for the flights were from the 13th

April to 20th April 1996, with myself and Mark flying from Manchester, whilst Haydn flew from one of the London airports. Apparently, the flight from Manchester became so over booked that it resulted in an additional flight being laid on, which both myself and Mark had the pleasure of flying on. God knows what time we departed but we actually made the 08.55 departure from Faro to Tavira, in time for Mark to enjoy his first CP Class 1800 when 1808 rolled in with the 08.55 Vila Real St Antonio **Guadiana** to Lagos as far as Faro. We had already purchased our weekly First-Class CP Rover tickets and on the return bumped into Haydn, who had arrived later than us on a flight from London. The weather was absolutely fantastic and this time I had packed a lightweight jacket plus plenty of Tee Shirts. The first day was spent covering CP 1200s, 1800s and 1931s before doing the overnight north from Faro to Pinhal Novo.

Left: 1807 departs Faro with the 08.35 from Barreiro.
Right: 1933 departs Tunes with the 14.15 Faro to Barreiro Rapido.

Prior to doing the overnight service to Barreiro, we took time out to visit a restaurant in Faro, to enable Mark and

Haydn to enjoy their first glasses of Portuguese beer and local food dishes and to be honest I think we all enjoyed the evening, especially the beer!

Then it was onto the platform at Faro in plenty of time prior to the arrival of our overnight service. That evening, 1808 appeared as expected and we quickly found two empty compartments for our journey north. I seem to recall having a very comfortable journey arriving in Pinhal Novo on time and in plenty of time for the first local service of the day.

Then we hit the first problem, unfortunately Mark mustn't have fully woken up and somehow managed to trip up as we crossed the tracks in front of the train we had arrived on. His fall, resulted in numerous cuts mainly to his hands but thankfully no broken bones. After using numerous cloths, we managed to sort out the worst of the cuts and were soon on our way to Setubal on 1462. From here we started a series of moves on various local services before dropping on mega rare 1202 at Setubal whilst working the 07.25 to Barreiro. The reason for its rarity was that the first four Class 1200's were mainly used on ECS duties at Barreiro. Then we dropped on even rarer Class 1901: 1902 at Pinhal Novo whilst working an IC Rapido, the 07.45 Baja to Barreiro, which was taken through to Barreiro.

CP 1202 at Setubal   1902 after arrival at Barreiro.

After arrival back at Barreiro, it was time to board our ferry across the river to Lisboa. This time the boat was named 'Algarve', which seemed appropriate considering we had travelled up from that region. Once across the river we headed directly to Lisboa SA station and took 2611 hauling the 11.00 Rapido service to Porto as far as Entrocamento.

With our First-Class tickets we were able to relax whilst Mark found time to clean himself up after his misadventure. From Entroncamento we returned south to Santarem on 2606 to pick up our first old electric of the trip when required 2556 worked the 12.00 Lisboa SA to Covilhã. The sight at Entroncamento of 1567 hauling the 13.20 to Badajoz didn't distract us from our plan, which involved heading further north up to Pampilhosa to cover two 1961 diagrams.

We took two IR services from Entrocamento to Pampilhosa, first with 5618 working the 12.05 Lisboa SA to Porto as far as

Coimbra B, then 5626 on the 13.03 Lisboa SA to Guarda. The latter would require a change of engines on arrival at Pampilhosa to a Canadian built 'Dumper Truck' 1970 which we took to Mortagua for another Dumper Truck: 1966 back to Pampilhosa whilst working the 15.20 Guarda to Lisboa SA. With our First-Class Rover Tickets, we had very little problems in finding empty seats, which made the trip more relaxing and enjoyable.

Left: 1970 at Pampilhosa on the IR service to Guarda.
Right: 1966 after arrival at Pampilhosa with a service from Guarda.

It was around this time we lost Haydn, who had decided to do some shack bashing, which basically involves him boarding and departing trains at different stations. Apparently, during this part of the trip Haydn, actually walked through a single bore railway tunnel to get to his next station. On our return to Pampilhosa we bumped into a friend of Marks, who gave us a quick update on that day's events before we continued south on our service to Lisboa with old electric 2508, which was taken through to Entroncamento. Then a series of moves at Abrantes before retiring for the night at the usual hotel opposite the station.

Left: 2508 at Pampilhosa   Right: 1453 stabled at Abrantes

The following day, we made a relatively early start from Entroncamento on the 07.05 to Alfarrerede which was an EMU to cover the inbound 1400 diagram the 05.08 from Elvas to Entroncamento, which thankfully had required 1456 on the front. We then headed back to Abrantes on 1947 hauling the 08.03 Lisboa SA to Covilhã. After which, a short leap to Alfarrerede on 1551 working the 09.00 Lisboa SA to Covilhã for 1554 working the 07.50 Covilhã back to Abrantes then forward on the same service from Abrantes through to Lisboa SA with old electric 2556.

Left: 2556 backs onto the service from Covilhã to Lisboa Sa.
Right: 1947 at Abrantes with 1453 alongside on the 09.50 to Badajoz

We decided to head back across the river to cover the diesel services working around Barreiro, this time we had the ferry named 'Lagos'. We spent the whole of the afternoon and evening covering the diesels in and out of Barreiro. Things got very excited when CP 1903 backed all the way into Barreiro station and appeared to be ready to work a service but at the last minute it headed off to the depot. By 22.05, we were once again heading over the river to Lisboa in plenty of time to catch the overnight service up to Porto. If I remember correctly, I think we had sufficient time to enjoy some food and beer before boarding our overnight service north to Porto with 2609 on the 00.06 departure to Porto.

Left: 1939 departs Barreiro with the 18.15 Rapido to Faro
Right: 1804 with the 19.35 service to Vila Real St Antonio Guadiana. Whilst 1806 on the right is the 19.40 service to Setubal.

At Porto we spent the early part of the morning covering as many of the CP 1400 diagrams as possible before Mark and myself found a building on the main platform that offered shower and washing facilities. So, after a thorough freshen up, we were once again on our way concentrating on the 1400s, before calling it a day and heading back down to Entroncamento for a night at the usual hotel.

The next day after a breakfast at the hotel we took required class leader CP 1931 on the 08.03 Lisboa SA to Covilhã from Entroncamento to Abrantes for required 1946 working the 07.15 Covilhã to Lisboa SA back to Entroncamento then went forward on the same service down to Lisboa SA with electric 5602. Then we once again headed north first with 2621 working the 12.05 to Porto then swopped onto 5614 whilst working 13.03 Lisboa SA to Guarda as far as Pampilhosa for some more Dumper Truck action. First of all, dud 1967 dropped onto our train, which we took forward to a place called Santa Comba Dao then returned to Pampilhosa on required 1963 working the 15.20 Guarda to Lisboa SA. Then it was time for a quick double back from Pampilhosa back to Santa Comba Dao on required 1558 working the 18.28 Coimbra to Guarda then a return Pampilhosa with 1559 working the 18.30 Guarda to Lisboa SA.

Left: 1963 after arrival at Pampilhosa
Right: 1558 at Pampilhosa with the 18.28 from Coimbra to Guarda.

Finally, we took 2629 from Pampilhosa back to Entroncamento where we had over three hours to kill, so we found a suitable bar to enjoy a meal and the odd beer before heading back to the station at about 02.00 am to board the overnight service from Lisboa SA to Porto, which was running 30 minutes late and taken through to Porto.

After covering as many of the CP 1400 diagrams as possible and picking up a CP Gronk at Porto Sao Bento station, it was time to head out east to Tua on the 10.48 Porto Sao Bento to Tua with 1414 at the business end. On route to Tua we stopped off at Régua to photograph a group of former narrow gauge steam engines that were slowly rusting away around a turntable located close to the station:

A total of nine former CP narrow gauge steam engines were dumped around a turntable close by the station at Régua.

After a short stay at Régua, we continued to Tua to enjoy a ride on the narrow-gauge line that links Tua to Mirandela. We took 9022 out to the crossing points on the line north to

Mirandela working the 14.10 north then changed onto 9021 working the 14.50 from Mirandela back to Tua. The line north is spectacular as the line is located on a ledge built into the rock face overlooking a river that flows south back to Tua. It was here I realised I had left my jacket on the train when we arrived at Tua. So immediately on my return, I visited the Lost Property office at the station. At first the guy denied any knowledge of my jacket but after some persistence he suddenly remembered that my jacket had been handed in. Suspect he fancied the jacket for himself but my determination won the day.

Left: Narrow gauge 9022 with the 14.10 Tua to Mirandela
Right: 9021 arrives at Vilarinho with the 14.50 Mirandela to Tua.

After the excitement of the narrow-gauge line, it was time to head back west to Porto ready for our second overnight experience. However, this was achieved via a series of double backs that enabled me to pick up another three CP Class 1400s: 1405, 1418, 1425 on route to Porto Campanha.

In the early hours of Friday 19th April, we caught the south bound overnight service from Porto Campanha at 01.02. We did the overnight down to Pampilhosa, arriving about 03.00 am, to cover a few services prior to catching the 05.20 Mangualde to Coimbra from Pampilhosa at 08.00 am, running 40 minutes late with Class 1400: 1450. This was taken through to Coimbra for a quick EMU back to the junction at Coimbra B. It was then the turn of 5600 Class leader: 5601 working the IC Rapido 07.50 Braga to Lisboa SA through to its destination.

At Lisboa we crossed the river Tagus to Barreiro on the ferry 'Algarve', for our final crossing of the river. We spent the day covering various local and long-distance services in and out of Barreiro. Suspect I got slightly excited when former Spanish Alco 1329 ran light engine into Barreiro station but to no avail, it then proceeded to run back to the depot.

1803 16.40 Barreiro – Praias-Sado

Final move of the afternoon was behind required 1507 whilst working the 17.35 Barreiro to Praias-Sado, which we took to Setubal.

1507 arrives at Barreiro with the ecs prior to working the 17.35.

Finally, myself and Mark had decided not to do the overnight south but to travel on the 18.15 Barreiro to Faro from Setubal with a very noisy 1944 providing the entertainment up front. As this was a CP Rapido service, we would have had to purchase a seat reservation, which I believe we did at Setubal. Then next stop was Tunes with an eventual arrival at Faro around 22.00 pm. We soon managed to book a hotel, then made the most of our last night on the Algarve in a local bar, prior to crashing out for the night.

You may have gathered at some point during the day we had once again lost Haydn, I later found out he did the overnight down to the Algarve with Class 1800: 1803, after being distracted by a 1400 working a Figueira da Foz service from Lisboa SA, which is understandable.

The following day, Saturday 20th April, myself and Mark caught a taxi from the hotel direct to the airport for our flight home on a Caledonian Tri-Star G-BBAE. This brought to an end to a very enjoyable week in Portugal with great company, beer and food, fabulous weather and most importantly, great engines!

One very amusing memory I have of one of my trips to Portugal, happened when myself and June were leaving Porto during October 1995. We were heading back south to Lisboa, whilst en route to the Algarve on an IC Rapido service. Just prior to our departure, a Portuguese woman came to us and told us in a very firm loud voice that we were in First Class coach, to which I replied 'Yes, I know, we have First Class Tickets'! She obviously had an issue with us, as she had walked half the length of the coach to try and put us in our place, only to be sent away complaining very loudly!

Then the train Guard came around to check the tickets prior to departure, only to find the woman and her husband didn't have First Class Tickets, so he ejected them out of the First-Class coach. Before she left, I went up to her and told her that Third Class was at the back of the train and in future don't annoy customers who are travelling First Class.

8 – Republic of Ireland

Soon after my first visit to Portugal during November 1994, I was persuaded to visit the Republic of Ireland by Lenny Ball, who had been to the country on a number of occasions. So, on Wednesday 28th December 1994, four of us headed over to Ireland, including myself, Lenny, Bert Heeley and his son Simon. This involved me driving from home and picking the others up en-route, eventually arriving in Holyhead around 23.00, in time to park the car and purchase a number of day return foot passenger tickets for the Ferry to Dun Laoghaire. If I remember correctly, the tickets cost around £9 for a day return. I think the Ferry departed soon after midnight and took about 5 hours to make the crossing. The crossing was fairly lively and caused a few of us to turn green. Eventually we arrived at Dun Laoghaire and were soon on our way, walking across to the railway station to purchase our Dublin Day Rover ticket, which I believe cost in the region of 5.5 Irish Punts (approximately £6.50) but if you paid in English 50p (i.e., the same coin as a half a Punt), you could get the ticket for £5.50. I would never have thought about doing that but Lenny Ball was well versed in these financial matters. The first diesels we saw following our arrival were a pair of IE Class 121s when 126 and 129 ran light engine through the station. We had no option other than to take an Iarnód Éirann (IE) Dart EMU from Dun Laoghaire station through to Dublin Pearse to pick up the 08.06 Pearce to

Drogheda service with an IE Class 121: 122 hauling a set of BR Built MK 3 coaches in push pull mode.

Left: 166 at Connolly station with the 06.56 Arklow to Drogheda.
Right: 080 at Connolly station with the 07.30 arrival from Rosslare.

The Dublin Day Rover ticket was an extremely useful ticket to use on your first trip to the Republic and during the morning we were taking full advantage of many local services that were loco hauled, which included:

166 - 06.56 Arklow to Drogheda
127 – 07.24 Drogheda to Pearse
170 – 09.35 Connolly to Rosslare
080 – 07.30 Rosslare to Connolly
113 – 11.00 Connolly to Belfast

We headed up to Skerries on a Dart service to cover the inbound 11.30 from Drogheda and were surprised to find an IE A Class: 012 working a south bound freight. The Class 001 or (A) were one of the earliest diesel locomotives classes that the Republic owned and built at the Metro Vickers works in Dukinfield, Manchester. A total of 60 locomotives were built during 1955 and 1956 and by the time of our visit only a handful of engines were still active and used mainly on freight services.

Left: A Class 012 at Skerries with a freight from a local quarry.
Right: 166 arriving at Skerries with the 11.30 Drogheda to Connolly.

The fast service between Dublin and Belfast were in the hands of Northern Ireland Class 111, which are virtually the same as the IE Class 071 i.e., built by General Motors in La Grange, Illinois, USA. At that time, 112 and 113 were both working the cross-border service. By the afternoon we were taking advantage of the Class 121s that worked the semi fast shuttle service between Pearse and Drogheda, which that day were: 122 and 124. The last move of the trip involved an out and back run from Connolly to Maynooth on the line to Sligo. These services were operated by IE Class 071s, with 084 working the 18.30 Connolly to Sligo for 082 on the return with the 17.40 Sligo to Connolly. This involved an hour stay in Maynooth, so a quick visit to one of the local pubs seemed appropriate and allowed us to enjoy a real glass of the black stuff. On our return to Dublin, we caught a

Dart service down to Dun Laoghaire then a short walk to board the evenings sailing across to Holyhead.

Left: 112 13.00 Dublin Connolly to Belfast at Connolly.
Right: 124 13.44 Pearse to Drogheda at Donabate.

The return Ferry from Dun Laoghaire to Holyhead was thankfully a much smoother journey and allowed most of us to catch up on lost sleep by crashing out on some bench seats on the Ferry. The trip must have been enjoyable as I made a couple more day returns trips to Ireland during February and April 1995.

Eventually, I decided a longer trip to Ireland was in order and on the 22nd June, I started a five-day trip and based myself for the entire trip down in Limerick at the infamous Boylan's B&B. This establishment was a regular haunt for enthusiasts and it wasn't unusual for the place to be fully booked with cranks from the UK.

For this trip I was accompanied with Bert Heeley and Lenny Ball and it involved catching the 23.12 Birmingham New Street to Holyhead from Crewe. The service was timed to enable customers to catch the overnight Ferry from

Holyhead. The train was hauled by 37429 and delivered me on time to Holyhead. If I remember correctly the Ferry was still one of the older boats prior to the introduction of the modern Stena HSS. We spent the early part of the morning around Dublin before walking across to Dublin Heuston station where we took the 09.10 Dublin Heuston to Tralee with new GM class leader 201 to the junction station at Ballybrophy. Here we changed trains onto the limited service that operated between Ballybrophy to Limerick with small GM 157 ready to work the 10.30 Ballybrophy to Limerick.

Left: 157 at Ballybrophy with the 10.30 service to Limerick
Right: 171 at Ennis with the 12.10 from Limerick. Bert is on the phot.

The journey to Limerick proved to be a very bumpy and made it virtually impossible to sit still in your seat as the coach lurched about on its journey south. Suspect the Ballybrophy to Limerick line wasn't maintained to main line standards or in fact to any standard. On arrival at Limerick, we were surprised to find small GM 171 ready to work the

12.10 to Ennis, which myself and Bert took to Ennis. So, a quick trip along the former westerly route to Athenry.

Left: 171 at Ennis whilst running around its train.
Right: A Class 003 on Limerick Shed.

Once back at Limerick, we popped across to Boylan's B&B to check in and drop off the contents of our bags in our allocated rooms. Then back to Limerick station for a series of moves including Class 121: 128 which was working the shuttles to Limerick Junction. To finish the first day off we did a few journeys on the relatively new Class 201s on the mainline to Dublin before our intended return to Limerick from the Junction on the 19.40 from Rosslare. However, this was for some unknown reason terminated at the Junction for a replacement bus back to Limerick then straight to Boylan's for a solid night's sleep.

The following day the 23rd June, must have been a Friday as our plans involved covering two Friday only services that should have both dropped small GM engines. After a wholesome breakfast we headed to the station to find 166 working the 08.05 to the Junction, 203 on the 08.25 to Dublin and required 148 on the 07.55 to Ballybrophy, so off to Ballybrophy it was. After a couple of moves on Class 201s to Portlaoise then onto Kildare to cover a couple of Class 071s working on the Dublin to Waterford circuit. The first was 084 working the 11.40 Dublin to Waterford which was taken to Athy for 081 working the 10.55 Waterford to Dublin, which delivered us back to Kildare. Here we took required 188 working the Fridays only 10.00 Tralee to Dublin through to Dublin Heuston station.

Left: 188 arriving at Kildare with the FO 10.00 Tralee to Dublin.
Right: 188 after arrival at Dublin Heuston station.

In theory the move to Dublin should have been perfect to drop us onto the Friday only 16.55 to Ballina which was booked to be worked by a pair of small GMs but for some unknown reason IE had allocated a single Class 071 to work the service that weekend. Apparently, the weight of the 071 would normally have restricted its use but on the day, they used 083 to haul the train out to Ballina on the Friday. This was taken to Portarlington then two further Class 201s delivered us back at Limerick with time to visit the depot. The staff at the depot were extremely helpful and couldn't do enough for us, including telling us what was booked to work the first two small GM diagrams the following morning from Limerick plus what was booked to arrive from Rosslare on the morning service. Which confirmed we required 184 on the diagram to the Junction plus 172 on the service from Rosslare.

Left: Three small GMs on Limerick depot including 150 & 157.
Right: Another photo of A Class 003 on Limerick depot.

So, the following morning 184 produced as quoted on the 08.05 to the Junction, which we took. Then the problem was how on earth do you get 172 on the Rosslare which was booked only to work as far as the Junction. I'd been warned about this problem in advance of the trip, and was told to speak to the station staff, to see if they could help. So, we quickly found one of the station staff and asked how we could get to Tipperary to pick up the inbound service from Rosslare. Without any hesitation, he replied 'Please wait, whilst I get my car' and true to his word he arrived with his car and myself and Bert were soon on our way to Tipperary, which wasn't so long a way after all! Our driver told us to see the signalman at the station to see if the train was late and also have a cup of tea. After giving the guy a couple of

Punt for our car ride, we were walking up the steps to speak to the signalman who just couldn't be more helpful! He confirmed our train was on time then made us all a mug of tea followed by a long informative chat about the railways in Ireland. The hospitality of the local people was fantastic and made you feel extremely comfortable and relaxed.

Left: 184 after arrival at the Junction with the 08.05 from Limerick. Right: The Signal Box at Tipperary.

As per the previous night's gen a small GM arrived on time with the morning service from Rosslare and was taken back to the junction. Then we spent a few hours travelling behind numerous hauled services, which included our first visit to the lovely City of Cork and a trip behind required GM 192 whilst working the 12.05 Tralee to Cork. By about 18.00, we had arrived at Ballybrophy to time to cover the small GM on the direct line to Limerick. Wrong, IE decided to swap 081 that arrived on the 17.40 Dublin to Limerick for the small GM i.e., 155 that should have worked the branch service. I still haven't got a clue, why IE decided to swap the engines, especially as the small GM was lighter and in theory more suitable to work the branch but ha, you're in Ireland and anything can happen.

Left: 192 at Mallow with the 12.05 Tralee to Cork.
Right: 155 at Ballybrophy with the 17.40 Dublin to Limerick.

The following day Sunday 25th June, was our last full day of the trip, so we decided to have a trip to Dublin before arriving back at Limerick Junction in time to take required small GM 168 working the 20.53 Limerick Junction to Limerick and call it a day.

After our full English breakfast washed down with plenty of tea, it was time to check out of our rooms. Then the usual stroll across to the station, typically, we needed both small GMs with 175 on the Ballybrophy and 141 on the front of the 08.05 to the Junction. We decided to take the class leader i.e., 141 as 175 looked like it was relatively ex works, so hopefully more of a chance to get it at a later date.

Left: 175 Prior to working the 07.55 to Ballybrophy.
Right: 141 Ready to work the 08.05 Limerick to the Junction.

After enjoying our ride behind 141, which was the one and only time I had a chance of it for haulage, we headed north to Dublin with 225 whilst working the 07.35 Cork to Dublin Heuston. After arriving at Heuston station we immediately headed over to Connolly station to see what was working. First train covered was required Class 121: 123 working the 11.05 Pearse to Drogheda which was taken to Skerries then 078 back to Connolly with the 11.26 Drogheda to Connolly service. Next, was our last return trip of the day with required NIR Class 111: 112 working the 13.00 Connolly to Belfast, which we took to Mosney before returning on required Class 071: 077 working the 15.04 Pearse to Mosney. At which point we headed for the Ferry across to Holyhead and the start of our journey home. This brought to an end our first multi day trip to Ireland and started a love affair with the country, until IE decided to replace most of their hauled services with modern Japanese built DMU's.

I did a couple more day trips across to the Republic before it was time to enjoy a four-day trip during March 1996. This trip had been arranged to coincide with an Irish Traction Group (ITG) railtour run on the 23rd March 1996 called 'The Yankee Explorer', more about that later.

On the night of the 19th March, I drove over to Holyhead to catch the night Ferry across to Dun Laoghaire. I then spent most of the day down in the lower half of the country and managed to have small GM 182 from Cork to Cobh on the 13.25 departure then back to Cork and finally up to Mallow on 182. After which I decided to head for Limerick to check into Boylan's B&B. The final train of the day was required small GM 158 from the Junction back to Limerick whilst working the 19.40 from Rosslare and departed the Junction at 23.12. The train had a number of enthusiasts on board, most of which headed directly to Boylan's.

The next day, I headed to the station to find small GM 162 on the 07.55 to Ballybrophy, whilst I took required 164 working the 08.05 to the Junction. From there, I headed south again and managed to find two small GM's: 177 working the 09.10 Cork to Tralee whilst 171 worked the 12.50 Cork to Tralee. At the time I couldn't think of a better way to enjoy my hobby other than travel behind small GMs in this very relaxing country.

Left: 164 at Limerick Jct, after arriving with the 08.05 from Limerick.
Right: 177 at Mallow with the 09.10 Cork to Tralee.

After spending sometime in a pub close to Thurles station, it was time to return to the Junction to meet 190 on the 19.40 Rosslare to Limerick. This time the train was full of cranks from the UK and again most of them headed over to Boylan's only to find the good lady herself stood outside the front door counting everybody into her B&B.

The next day I headed down to the breakfast room and found it full of cranks from the UK, most had obviously come over to travel on the ITG railtour on the Saturday. At about 07.40 a couple arrived in the breakfast room, to find the room full, at which point everyone got up and quickly exited the room. I told the couple that they were all heading to the station to catch a train to Dublin, as they appeared shocked at the sight of everyone leaving.

This time I had the option of either 192 to Ballybrophy (see photo on page 108) or 162 to the Junction, which I took.

Then, swiftly up to Dublin and across to Connolly station. I soon bumped into friends Pete Yarwood and Haydn Pollitt and spent the day covering various services, which included, 142 & 157 working the 16.32 Connolly to Drogheda and 149 on the 17.15 Connolly to Longford. We finished the day back on 142 & 157 whilst working the 17.48 Drogheda to Connolly then I suspect a Dart EMU down to Dun Laoghaire.

Both Photos: 142 & 157 with the 16.32 Connolly to Drogheda.

After checking in at the pre-booked B&B and dumping our bags in our room, myself, Pete and Haydn visited a few local pubs in the town before crashing out for the night.

The following day was the day of the ITG railtour which started at Dublin Heuston at 06.05 am before heading to Bray on the coast. Here, the tour reversed and stopped at Dun Laoghaire at 07.35 where we boarded the train.

Left: 112 whilst heading to Portadown on the 'The Yankee Explorer'
Right: 111 prior to being attached to the tour at Portadown.

At Portadown 112 was joined with 111 to work the railtour to Lisburn, then IE small GMs 130 and 135 continued with the train to Londonderry before reversing and returning to Belfast Gt. Victoria Street station. Here, the sole surviving Hunslet built Class 101: 102 would haul the train the short distance from Belfast Gt. Victoria Street Belfast Central.

Left 130 and 135 after arrival at Londonderry.
Right: NIR 102 at Belfast Gt. Victoria Street station.

Then, NIR recently acquired Class 201 diesels 208 and 209 hauled the train down to Portadown via a quick visit to the Carriage sidings at York Road. At Portadown, 208 continued on its own to Connolly for IE Class 071: 081 forward to Dun

105

Laoghaire. On arrival at Dun Laoghaire, virtually the whole train emptied and made their way across to the Port to board the evening sailing to Holyhead. This brought to an end a thoroughly enjoyable short visit to the Republic and Northern Ireland.

On the 19th October 1996, a group of us booked on the ITG 'The Euro-Port & lemon Railtour', which we decided to cover during a single day visit the Republic. After doing the early part of the tour from Dun Laoghaire to Bray then reverse back up to Dublin Connolly with Class 071: 084, we opted to get off the railtour whilst it visited the branch at Navan. This allowed us to cover a number of local services that proved very useful as required small GM 183 worked the 06.57 Arklow to Connolly and then we had required Class 121: 129 working the 09.07 Connolly to Maynooth and return on the 10.05 Maynooth to Connolly.

Left: 183 after arrival at Connolly with the 06.57 from Arklow.
Right: 129 at Maynooth with the 09.07 from Connolly.

By 11.30 am we had re-joined the railtour at Connolly and headed south to Rosslare Harbour with NIR 112.

Left NIR 112 at Wexford during a photo stop.
Right: A copy of the Railtour Programme.

Unfortunately, the planned use of Class 121, 141 and 181s on the railtour didn't happen and NIR 112 continued with the train until the end of the day, which saw us getting off at Dun Laoghaire prior to catching the Ferry back to Holyhead. I appreciate things can go wrong when running a railtour as I've been in that situation myself on a number of times but to be honest the none availability of the smaller GM diesels seriously put a dampener on the whole day.

After this, I still found time for a number of day trips to Ireland plus two further three-day trips during July and November 1997. Unfortunately, by this time I had dipped my toe into Belgium and Germany, which began to completely dominate my plans for trips abroad, helped by the availability of regular flights from Manchester to Brussels and Dusseldorf.

Left: 124 at Connolly 10.40 to Enfield on the 5th November 1996.
Right: 122 and 189 at Connolly with the 10.55 Drogheda to Pease.

192 at Limerick with the 07.55 to Ballybrophy, 22nd March 1996.

9 – Belgium and Luxembourg

Whilst enjoying railtours in the UK and visits to places like Ireland the subject of bashing in Belgium and Luxembourg regularly popped up in the conversation. Many of my friends were very familiar with both countries and it didn't take long before I had hatched plans for my first visit. Haydn Pollitt had briefed me on places to concentrate my visit, which usually involved areas that provided plenty of diesel haulage and old electrics locomotives working on passenger services.

My first trip involved flying out on Tuesday 11th June and returning 5 days later on Sunday 16th June 1996. I had been advised to purchase a 5-day Benelux Tourrail Rover ticket. So, after booking my flights with BA, I was soon on the 19.25 departure from Manchester to Brussels on G-BKYH a B737-200 series jet and landed in Brussels before 22.00 pm and made a service into the centre of Brussels and immediately went to the ticket office at Brussels Centraal station to purchase my Rover Ticket. The guy I spoke to at the ticket office couldn't understand why I had left the UK as the UEFA 1996 football championship had only just started in the UK on the 8th June. At least, we spoke the same language and within minutes I had obtained my 5-Day Benelux Rover ticket and was soon heading down to Liege to travel on a couple of overnight trains that operated between Paris and Dortmund. The first part of this involved boarding the 22.42 Dortmund to Paris which I thought had a SNCB Class 27 on the front until I noticed the same engine pass the coach I was sat in as the train departed Liege Guillemin en route to Namur. So, God knows what hauled the train to Namur other than it was more than likely a Class 22 or 23 electric. The service arrived at Namur on time and it wasn't long before the 23.22 Paris to Dortmund overnight service arrived with 2204 at 03.25 am which was taken back to Liege. Most of the stock used on these overnights were old German compartment stock with seats that folded down to form effectively a bed in the compartment. Needless to say, at that time of the night, the compartments were regularly used as sleeping berths but I had to avoid falling into a deep sleep, otherwise you could find yourself in France!

After spending some time back at Liege, I headed north to Gent St Pieters station to cover the many diesel services that worked in that area. These included the services to Ronse, Geraardsbergen and Eeklo.

Left: 6315 departs Eine with the 10.52 Gent St Pieters to Ronse
Right: 6202 departs De Pinte station with the 11.09 Ronse to Gent.

After Gent St Pieters, I took SNCB Class 12: 1203 from Gent across to Antwerp Centraal to cover the latter part of the afternoon rush there. The move out to Berchem involved SNCB Class 25: 2506 for 2503 onto Lier, from where I covered five different Class 62 diagrams including: 6245, 6295, 6281, 6299 and 6240 before taking 1185 whilst working the 18.30 Amsterdam to Brussels Midi from Antwerp to Brussels Noord.

Left: 2506 departs Berchem with the 16.55 Antwerp to Turnhout.
Right: 6281 arriving at Olen with the 18.22 Neerpelt to Antwerp.

From Brussels, I headed down to Liege Guillemins and immediately checked into the Univers Hotel located across from the station. After a few beers I had time for a quick out and back to Angleur with 5510 paired with 5523 working the 22.45 Liege Guillemins to Gouvy followed by 5515 working the 20.48 Luxembourg to Liege.

The following day I did a series of moves between Liege Guillemins and Herstal including plenty of visits to Jonfosse and Palais stations. The day started with getting a Liege Banker on the 05.32 Welkenraedt to Brussels with 2752 on the front but more importantly Dot Class 55: •5532 banking on the rear all the way to Ans. The Dot before the number indicates the engine had no boiler or electric train heating facilities.

Left: 5513 at Liege Jonfosse station with the 06.16 from Gouvy.
Right: 5528 at Herstal station with the 08.18 from Gouvy.

After 5528, I headed back north to Antwerp and spent most of the day there before a visit to Gent St Pieters to have Class 62s: 6206, 6247, 6304 and 6322. Then I took 2741 down to Liege to complete another overnight on the services from Paris to Dortmund. This time noting the engine on the front prior to departure from Liege, which was 2350 working the 22.42 Dortmund to Paris. I must have been mega desperate as on my return from Namur, I left Liege Guillemins at 04.24 on the 03.49 Welkenraedt to Ostende service to experience my first ever Brussels morning rush hour and introduced me to a completely new world of bashing, utter madness! During the morning I made sure of covering the booked Class 51 diagram, 06.47 Ronse to Schaarbeek which was worked by 5104, one of the regular performers on this diagram. The noise of it passing through the rail tunnels underneath Brussels was well worth it and must have regularly upset many of the commuters as they stood on the adjoining platforms.

After Brussels, it was the time to visit Charleroi to cover a number of Class 62 diagrams plus any old electric diagrams before I had my first SNCB Class 18: 1801 working the 17.08 Koln HBF to Paris. Finally, a quick out and back from Namur to Brussels with two Class 20's i.e., 2010 working the 10.25 Milan to Brussels Midi and finally 2025 working the 22.16 Brussels Midi to Basel overnight which dropped me off at Namur around 23.30. The Class 20s had the nickname of Spaceships and certainly sounded impressive!

Left: 2628 at Namur with the 17.08 Namur to Charleroi.
Right: SNCN 1801 at Charleroi with the Koln to Paris EC service.

I had earlier in the day checked into the Hotel Queen Victoria in Namur, which would become a regular haunt for me in years to come plus home for many enthusiasts from the UK. Namur was definitely the place to be on a Saturday morning during the summer as SNCB operated a number of weekend services hauled by Nohab diesels including Class, 52s, 53s and 54s from Namur to the Ardennes. These enabled hundreds of locals to enjoy the countryside and the opportunity to Kayak on the river that passed through the region. These services were known as the 'Kayaks'.

After a well-earned sleep at the Queen Vic, it was time for breakfast including plenty of strong black coffer prior to my first ride on a Nohab diesel. •5312 was provided at Namur for the run down to Houyet then runs behind 5401 and •5211 were enjoyed.

Left: •5312 after arrival at Houyet with the 08.25 from Namur.
Right: •5211 at Dinant with the 10.30 to Bertrix.

The Kayaks quickly became a magnet for enthusiasts from the UK, with many travelling over to Belgium at the weekend to simply ride behind them. By late morning, I was heading back over to Liege to see what was on the 12.10 to Luxembourg, which was a very dud 5515, so off to Gent to spend the afternoon there. After a series of Class 62's, it was time to cover the summer dated service from the coastal resort of Blankenberge i.e., 19.51 Blankenberge to Quevy, which was usually hauled by a Charleroi allocated Class 51 but, on this occasion appeared with Charleroi allocated •6217 and 6290. So off to Zottegem with the pair then 6201 working a service back to Gent.

Left: 6290 & •6217 depart Zottegem with the Blankenberge to Quevy, whilst Haydn waits on the platform.
Right: 6201 at Zottegem with the 20.46 Geraardsbergen to Gent.

After the excitement of the pair of Class 62s, I headed back to Liege to do another overnight this time to Verviers as the overhead power was scheduled to be switched off to the east of Liege forcing SNCB to use diesels on the overnights, resulting in both •5502 and 5535 working the overnights. 5521 worked an additional overnight towards Germany.

By now it was Sunday 16th June 1996, so I headed north from Liege and had the pleasure of my first banking turn behind 2383, which was one of the dedicated engines for banking duties up the steep climb to Ans. As this was the last day and my flight scheduled for a 17.00 pm departure from Brussels, I decided to spend some time back at Antwerp and was rewarded when •6207 worked the 09.22 Neerpelt to Antwerp.

Left: •6207 with the 09.22 Neerpelt to Antwerp.
Right: 6261 at Antwerp Centraal with the 11.09 to Neerpelt.

At this time SNCB had just started the massive project of converting the terminus at Antwerp into a multi levelled station with the lower level providing a through route for services to and from the Netherlands.

By 17.00 pm I was heading home on my scheduled BA flight from Brussels to Manchester. In those days, Manchester was a huge operating hub for BA. However, their senior management soon put an end to all those convenient flights when they made the decision to close down their operations at Manchester and concentrate virtually all their business at Heathrow.

This was the end of a very enjoyable but exhausting 5-day trip to Belgium, which I must have enjoyed, so much so that I would soon be planning another visit to start on the 22nd August.

Belgium was a completely different challenge when compared to visits to Portugal and the Republic of Ireland. The latter two offered you a more relaxed type of trip with plenty of time for beers and longer journeys but Belgium was just basically full on and for some people a physical challenge by doing solid overnights for the whole of the trip. I eventually got into a pattern of staying at Namur, which was a very pleasant place to base yourself. Then do a couple of early morning commuter moves around Namur before either heading over to Liege to cover a full morning rush hour there or slowly working your way up to Brussels covering numerous old electric diagrams whilst en route and avoided doing a full Brussels morning rush hour.

As mentioned, my next trip to Belgium started with a BA flight from Manchester to Brussels, then the usual overnight move via Liege to Namur. The Paris to Dortmund and return overnights were that night both SNCB Class 22's: 2239 for 2230 back from Namur. When 5537 dropped onto the back of the 05.32 Welkenraedt to Brussels Midi, I opted to head up to Brussels and managed to pick up 5105 on the 06.47 Ronse to Schaarbeek diagram. By 10.00 am I had arrived in Zottegem and very pleased to see 5111 working the 09.46 Geraardsbergen to Gent St Pieters, which I believe was a booked Class 51 diagram at the time.

Left: 5111 at Gent St Pieters after arriving from Geraardsbergen.
Right: 6219 Green livery with the 12.07 Gent St Pieters to Eeklo.

After covering most of the day time Class 62 diagrams around Gent, it was time to head down to Brussels to enjoy the delights of an afternoon rush hour there. To be honest, it was a smart move as I found 5103 on the 16.21 Schaarbeek to Ronse then north to Mechelen to have •5116 working the 16.15 Leuven to Dendermonde.

Left: 5103 at Schaarbeek with the 16.21 to Ronse.
Right: •5116 at Kapelle Op working the 16.21 from Leuven. Note the missing '•' on the front of 5116 but visible on the cab side number.

After the pair of 51s, it was down to Namur with 2021 working the 19.13 Brussels Midi to Milan overnight for another night at the Queen Vic. I seem to recall visiting a local bar not far from the hotel and slowly getting wasted on some seriously strong beer.

The next day was a Saturday, so time to do the Kayaks and found 5403 working the 08.25 Namur to Houyet, followed by 5401 whilst •5307 worked the 10.30 Dinant to Bertrix.

Left: 5403 at Houyet after working the 08.25 from Namur.
Right: •5307 at Dinant with the 10.30 to Bertrix.

119

After covering all three Nohab diagrams, I headed over to Liege to see which diesels were working and fell on 5523, 5529 and finally •5508, which made it a worthwhile visit. Then up to Gent St Pieters, to see what was working off the coast and was very pleased to find 5150 working the 19.51 Blankenberge to Quevy, which was taken to Ath.

Another rancid overnight down at Liege but this time it included a SNCB Gronk i.e., 8229 on shunt release at Verviers. I spent most of the day covering the Diesels on the Neerpelt line then across to Gent St Pieters before taking SNCB 1802 whilst working the 13.34 Ostende to Koln EC service. Then it was the turn of dud Class 20: 2006 from Brugge to Namur direct whilst working the 19.02 Blankenberge to Arlon and avoiding Brussels.

Left: 1802 at Gent St Pieters with the 13.34 Ostende to Koln HBF.
Right: 1806 waits its next service at Ostende.

Another evening was spent in the usual bar close to the hotel then back to the Queen Vic for some doss.
As the following day was a Monday, a normal working day, you needed to be up early to cover the first morning commuter trains. So, early, you couldn't enjoy a Breakfast

but thankfully the night porter would provide a couple of flasks of very strong black coffee in the breakfast area, which was gratefully received. The coffee certainly helped with getting my brain into gear.

First move of the day was an EMU out west to Ronet to pick up required 2326 working the 04.58 Charleroi to Namur. Then another EMU over to Statte have 2335 on the 06.36 Statte to Liers, which was taken to Liege, passing 2351 on the 07.01 Huy to Brussels Midi whilst en route and 5508 arriving with the 06.16 Gouvy to Herstal.

Left: 2335 after arrival at Liege Guillemins with the 06.36 from Statte.
Right: 5508 at Liege Guillemins with the 06.16 Gouvy to Herstal.

Then required SNCB 1804 appeared on the 06.30 Koln HBF to Brussels Midi, which was taken to Brussels Noord, helped by the fact that required 5536 banked the heavily loaded train up the steep gradient to Ans. I didn't hang around Brussels too long before heading up to Gent St Pieters to cover the diesels, which included: 6204, 6213, 6237, 6301,

6392 and 6393. After which I travelled down to Leuven to see what was on the 16.15 to Dendermonde and I was rewarded with •5110 and taken to Mechelen. After a quick return to Brussels, I fell on SNCB Class 26: 2619 working the 17.05 Brussels Midi to Huy, which I took to Gembloux for 2007 forward to Namur whilst working the 16.56 from Schaarbeek to Namur rush hour service.

Left: 6301 14.05 Gent St Pieters to Geraardsbergen with 6393 & 6392.
Right: •5110 at Leuven with the 16.15 to Dendermonde.

From Namur I fell on my first SNCB Class 15: 1503 on the 17.03 Koln HBF to Paris across to Charleroi to cover three diesel diagrams: 6218, 6221 and 6271 before taking my second SNCB Class 15: 1505 from Charleroi to Liege Guillemins working the 21.01 Paris to Berlin overnight. This put me in position on my last day of the trip to once again do an out back from Liege to Namur with 2228 and 2203 working the two overnights, not ideal on the last night but it had to be done. I didn't stay long in Liege and went north to Brussels before heading to Zottegem to find •5112 working the 09.46 Geraardsbergen to Gent St Pieters, massive result.

Left: 1503 at Namur with the 17.08 Koln HBF to Paris.
Right: •5112 at Gent St Pieters with the 09.46 from Geraardsbergen.

Once I had covered all the diesels at Gent St Pieters, I headed east to Antwerp to check out the diesels working to Neerpelt. The final moves of the trip included required 5107 working the 16.15 Leuven to Dendermonde and 2618 working the 16.46 Brussels Midi to Leuven then it was time to head to the airport for the 20.10 Brussels to Manchester BA flight home with B737-200 G-BKYP. This was in the days when BA had just started to use unusual designs on the tail of their aircraft, until a famous Prime Minister mocked the idea during a press conference, exit fancy BA artwork.

Trips to Belgium started to happen quick and fast with the next one booked to start on Tuesday evening 1st October until the 6th October 1996 and had been arranged to coincide with the Belgium TTB day (Trains, Trams and Buses). Once a year the Belgium government tried to encourage its citizens to use public transport and as a means of inducement, they offered a full weekend of free travel on their public transport systems to anyone including foreigners like myself. What a novel idea, I won't even ask the question, why this doesn't happen in the UK!!

The 19.25 pm BA flight from Manchester, was G-BGDK: B737-200 series and not long after 22.30 pm I was jumping off a service at one of the stations underneath Brussels. I took the 22.34 Ostende to Welkenraedt through to Liege Guillemins and opted to visit a food outlet across from the station before boarding the overnight from Dortmund to Paris to Namur with required SNCB Class 23: 2331.

Left 5118 at Zottegem with 09.46 Geraardsbergen to Gent St Pieters.
Right: 5118 at Gent St Pieters after its arrival from Geraardsbergen.

After arriving back at Liege with the overnight bound for Dortmund, I headed north and spent a short time around Brussels prior to heading to Zottegem to have 5118 working the 09.46 Geraardsbergen to Gent St Pieters. Then covered the Class 62s around Gent before heading to Leuven to find required 5124 working the 16.15 to Dendermonde followed by 2340 working the 16.46 Brussels Midi to Leuven. I

124

finished the day with a quick visit to Charleroi and found two required Class 62s working the services to Couvin including: 6231 and 6285. Then it was 2235: 18.58 Paris to Namur, which I took through to Namur and headed direct to the Queen Vic for some well-earned sleep.

Left:6231 at Charleroi with the 20.14 to Couvin.
Right: 6285 at Charleroi with the 19.41 arrival from Couvin.

By now my early start from Namur started to work well and involved first viewing the engine that would pass through Namur to later work the 06.14 Dinant to Namur, which was on this occasion dud 2615. I then did 2314 from Namur to Flawinne working the 05.19 Namur to Charleroi for 2357 back to Namur with the 04.58 Charleroi to Namur.
I'm sure it was on this occasion that Andy Read was also staying at the Queen Vic but didn't appear in the morning as usual for the black coffee. I got the guy on reception to call Andy, who had over dossed and had about 5 minutes to make the 05.19 to Charleroi. Somehow, he managed to make it, whilst I held the rear door of the last coach open for him as he legged it down the platform and made the train

with seconds to spare. Obviously too much beer the night before. After the excitement of Namur, I headed up to Brussels to find required 5122 on the 06.47 Ronse to Schaarbeek which I had all the way from Brussels Noord to Schaarbeek!

Left: 6311 at Gent St Pieters with the 11.05 to Geraardsbergen.
Right: 5149 at Brussels Midi whilst being hauled to depot for attention.

After my visit to Gent St Pieters, I headed south to Charleroi to cover the afternoon rush hour services there. Owing to the lack of required engines on the stack at Charleroi station, myself and Andy spent most of the afternoon sat in the station bar located alongside the main platform whilst enjoying the odd beer!

By 16.25 we managed to drag ourselves from the bar when required 2356 produced on the 16.25 to Namur then straight back to Charleroi to cover a couple of Class 62s on the service to Couvin.

Left: 2356 at Couillet with the 16.25 Charleroi to Namur, whilst Andy checks our next move options.
Right: 6224 at Charleroi with the 15.47 P train to Couvin.

We later managed to have 2605 working the 17.08 Namur to Charleroi from Couillet back to Charleroi then two Class 15s: 1502 working the 16.34 Paris to Dortmund for 1504 working the 17.08 Koln HBF to Paris. I finally headed across to Liege and checked into the Univers Hotel for some much-needed sleep.

The next day, I covered most of the P trains around Liege, with only 2607 of any-note, working the 05.56 Jamelle to Liers. Later I managed to get my last but one SNCB Class 18: 1805 whilst working the 07.14 from Koln HBF to Ostende. Followed by two new Class 62s at Gent St Pieters i.e., 6307 working the 12.05 to Geraardsbergen then 6233 working the 12.46 Geraardsbergen to Gent St Pieters. Before heading down to Brussels to cover the afternoon rush hour and I managed to pick up three Class 26s: 2619 16.17 Vilvoorde to Nivelles, 2626 16.46 Brussels Midi to Leuven and finally 2630 17.04 Schaarbeek to Chatelet. We finally finished the day at Berchem close to Antwerp, where a group of us decided to visit a local bar and kill some time prior to joining the 22.15 Amsterdam to Paris overnight down to Mons. Here we visited a city centre bar for a couple of hours before boarding the north bound 23.22 Paris to Amsterdam overnight at the unearthly time of 04.04 am.

On arrival back at Berchem, it was now TTB day on Saturday 5th October and time to cover a number of Class 62s including: 6299, 6317 and 6295 in a pair, 6255 and 6267 before we arrived at Olen to catch the main engine of the day, preserved diesel 5910 which had been assigned to work an additional service at 07.52 from Mol to Dinant. To be honest I should have travelled much further on 5910, an engine that was built during 1954 by Cockerill at their Belgium factory at Seraing. But the knowledge that an Antwerp Dam Class 51 was booked to work an additional to Blankenberge blew any thoughts of that to pieces. The Class 59 was taken to Herentals for 5156 working the 07.33 Neerpelt to Blankenberge.

Left: 5910 at Herentals with the TTB special to Dinant.
Right: 5156 at Lier with the 07.33 Neerpelt to Blankenberge.

After getting off 5156 at Lier, I took required 6267 on the 09.09 Antwerp to Weert. Weert is in the Netherlands and was another bonus of TTB, with SNCB services to Neerpelt, extended to Weert. Then it was the turn of 5105 back to Antwerp Centraal and continued across to Gent St Pieters to check out the Class 62s and Class 12s. Finally, I took 1201 working the 13.05 Lille to Antwerp Centraal across to Antwerp before heading down to Liege to check into the Univers Hotel again. Here a group of us decided to finish the night off in one of the bars that in those days was directly opposite Guillemins station. This had been my first experience of a TTB day which proved to be a good one.

The following day, Sunday the 6th October and my last day in Belgium, so I didn't get too adventurous. I managed to have 5520 banking SNCB Class 16: 1602 up the hill to Ans whilst working the 06.30 Koln HBF to Brussels Midi. 2383 was also involved in Banking duties that day.

Left: 2383 just about to bank a service up the hill to Ans.
Right: 5523 at Liege Guillemins with the 13.08 to Luxembourg.

I did manage to get my last required SNCB Class 18: 1803 whilst working an Ostende to Koln HBF EC service from Liege Guillemins to Verviers. I finally departed Liege on the 11.14 Koln HBF to Ostende with Class 16: 1608 with 2383 banking the train to Ans.

By 17.00 I was safely on board the BA flight to Manchester with G-BKYP a B737-200 series.

My next trip to Belgium wasn't until March 1997, which would include my first visit to Luxembourg. I departed Manchester on the 24th March and would return home on the 30th March 1997. This time I opted to avoid doing the overnight at Liege, instead had prebooked a couple of nights at the Queen Vic, Namur. I actually made the 22.16 Brussels Midi to Basel overnight at Midi with spaceship 2012.

The coaches on these overnights had seriously comfortable seats and could easily lure you into falling asleep, net result you find yourself waking up in the wrong country.

Staying in the same hotel for a couple of nights, allowed me to dump some of my things in my bedroom, which certainly helped. The following day, I was up early and after a few cups of black coffee I walked across to the station to view what was heading to Dinant, as this was required 2344, it determined my early morning moves. First 2359 was taken working the 05.19 Namur to Charleroi to Floreffe. Here the station staff insisted that all passengers for Namur stay in a waiting room located in the main station building until the service arrived which was hauled by required 2334 on the 04.58 Charleroi to Namur. Back at Namur I took an EMU to Jambes Est then walked down the hill to Jambes to board the 06.14 Dinant to Namur with 2344. I then headed north to Brussels via Gembloux and had required 2366 from there to Brussels Noord whilst working the 07.01 Huy to Brussels Midi. Later that morning I had 2612 on the 07.08 Quevy to Schaarbeek then it was the turn of SNCB Class 18: 1802 from Brussels to Gent St Pieters to see 5109 arrive with the 09.46 from Geraardsbergen. Later, I took the 17.05 Brussels Midi to Huy from Brussels Noord down to Namur with required 2604. Then Class 15: 1503 across to Charleroi to do an out and back to Jamiouix with 6277 working the 20.14 Charleroi to Couvin, which departed 10 late, making a very tight connection at Jamiouix, thankfully I made required 6234 working the 19.41 Couvin to Charleroi. Then finally, 2229 working the 18.58 Paris to Namur, which was taken to its destination, as it was 37 mins late departing Charleroi, no time for beers.

The following day, I was up early once again to view dud 2605 heading down to Dinant, so no need to hang around for that. The usual out and back to Floreffe with required 2336 heading west for dud 2344 on the return to Namur. I must have done an EMU across to Liege Palais and dropped on required 2365 working the 06.56 Liers to Statte.

Left: 2365 at Liege Jonfosse with the 06.56 Liers to Statte.
Right: •5524 banking on the rear of 06.30 Koln HBF to Brussels Midi.

I departed Liege with Class 16: 1601 working the 06.30 Koln HBF to Brussels Midi with required •5524 banking the train to Ans. Time was spent at Gent St Pieters and Charleroi before a quick out and back from Namur to Ronet with two required Class 23's: 2328 17.08 Namur to Charleroi then 2364 back from Ronet with the 16.25 Charleroi to Namur.

Left: 2328 at Ronet with the 17.08 Namur to Charleroi. Note my bag!
Right: 2364 at Namur after arriving with the 16.25 from Charleroi.

By 18.55, I was heading south from Namur on SNCB Class 21: 2107 working the 17.54 Brussels Midi to Luxembourg in the company of Haydn Pollitt. This was my first visit to this relatively small country. I had been advised to stay at the

Carlton Hotel, which was managed by a fantastic guy called 'Johnny', who was well known to most Bashers who visited this lovely country. By about 21.00 pm we had safely arrived and quickly made our way to the Carlton and met the man himself who always referred to English Rail Enthusiast as British Railways.

The following day Thursday 27th March, we were both up relatively early to cover as many of the CFL Class 3600 diagrams as possible. These French Built centre cab electrics were built during the late 1950's and were affectionately known as Flat Irons. First task of the day, purchase a CFL day rover ticket which were incredibly cheap at about £3.50.

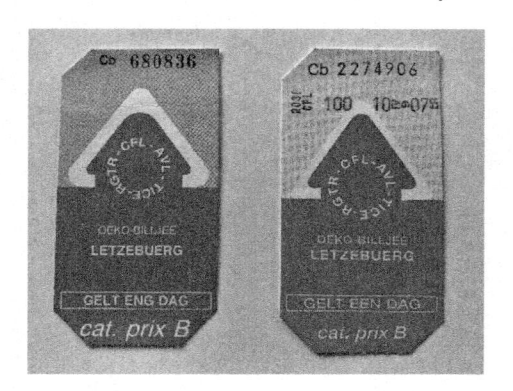

Left: Two CFL day rover tickets, the left ticket still unused.
Right: The Business card for the Carlton Hotel.

My first Flat Iron was 3618 working the 06.00 Luxembourg to Rumelange which I took to Bettembourg then 3613 06.21 Luxembourg to Petange to Esch/Alzette then 3619 working the 06.42 Petange to Luxembourg back to Bettembourg and finally SNCF Class 16000: 16681 working the 06.21 Nancy to

Luxembourg. Then a quick out and back to Hollerich with 3610 working the 06.40 Troisvierges to Hollerich for an EMU back to Luxembourg. At which point, it was time to head back to the hotel to enjoy a wholesome breakfast including as many boiled eggs as you could possibly eat all washed down with plenty of Orange juice and coffee. Johnny would always make you feel very welcome and was fluent in at least 5 different languages. His ability to switch language as he passed from table to table during breakfast was simply astonishing.

Left: 3609 at Ettelbruck with the 10.35 Luxembourg to Troisvierges. Right: 3617 at Rodange with the 12.10 Luxembourg to Rodange.

Luxembourg, was a truly international railway with trains arriving from surrounding countries including: France, Germany and Belgium.

After breakfast, I continued to chase Flat Irons and managed to have two CFL Class 1800 diesels: 1816 working the 13.27 Kleinbettingen to Luxembourg plus 1805 working the 15.30 Luxembourg to Trier.

Left: 1816 arrives at Capellen with the 13.27 from Kleinbettingen.
Right: 1805 at Luxembourg with the 15.30 service to Trier, Germany.

Left: 3606 at Luxembourg with the 14.04 from Troisvierges with Haydn just managing to sneak onto the photo.
Right: SNCF 15059 at Luxembourg with the 17.24 to Paris.

By 20.00 pm I was heading back north to Namur with required SNCB Spaceship: 2011. The train was the 10.25 Milan to Brussels Midi which I took to Namur and stayed at the Queen Vic. Whilst Haydn continued north to Brussels to presumably do another overnight.

Friday 28th March 1997, started as usual with an out and back to Floreffe with dud Class 23s: 2328 and 2344. Then across to Liege to cover P trains during the morning rush hour in addition to a number of Class 55s working mainly Luxembourg services. These included: 5523, 5525, 5531 plus 5531 and 5519 working the 11.08 Liege to Luxembourg which I took down to Aywaille for required 5505 working the 10.10 Luxembourg to Liege.

Left: 5519 at Liege Guillemins prior to 5531 dropping on the front.
Right: 2615 at Schaarbeek with the 17.04 to Chatelet.

After visits to Brussels and Charleroi it was time to return to Namur for another two nights at the Queen Vic. As this Easter, SNCB would be running additional services to the Ardennes. After enjoying my breakfast at the Queen Vic, it was across the road to see what was on the 08.25 to Houyet and thankfully it was required Nohab 5212 which was taken to Houyet. From here it was •5305 working the 08.32 Libramont to Dinant and finally 5205 working the 10.30 Dinant to Bertrix which was taken through to its destination.

Left: 5212 at Houyet with the 08.25 from Namur with boiler working.
Right: •5305 at Dinant with the 08.25 Libramont to Dinant

From Bertrix we took a single car SNCB DMU 4501 working the 12.00 Bertrix to Libramont for an IC service back up to Brussels Centraal. I finally, ended up at the coast at Blankenberge to check out the holiday dated service to Arlon, which thankfully that day had a required SNCB Spaceship. Here a number of us gathered for a photo opportunity in front of 2008, which was taken to Namur.

Left: SNCB: 2008 with Simon, Dave Pinfold, Chris Parkinson, Robin Havenhand and myself. Andy Read Photo.

Right: The same as above but with Andy replacing myself on the right.

The service to Arlon avoided Brussels and headed direct to Namur and arrived earlier enough for a group of us to enjoy the odd glass of beer in one of the local watering holes.

The next day was Easter Sunday and again SNCB ran a number of additional services to the Ardennes mainly using engines from the previous day including 5212 on the 08.25 Namur to Houyet and 5305 08.32 Libramont to Dinant with 5401 on the rear. As can be seen from the photos, both Nohab diesels had their steam boilers operating.

Left: 5212 after arrival at Houyet
Right: 5401 at Dinant after arriving with 5305 from Libramont.

Then it was time to head north and pick up anything that was required before it was time to head to the airport for the 17.00 BA flight to Manchester, G-BGDJ: B737-200 which brought to an end another very successful trip including my first visit to Luxembourg.

To conclude this chapter regarding visits to Benelux countries, I thought it only right to detail a trip that five of us made to visit Belgium, Germany and Luxembourg during July 1999. The group included myself, my partner Sheila, Paul Morris aka Bod with his partner Siobhan and finally Derek

Marcroft. We flew out from Manchester to Brussels on the 15th July and returned home on the 25th July 1999.

We had booked into a hotel close to Brussels Midi station which was unfortunately infested with cockroaches which wasn't a good start to the trip. However, after checking in to the hotel we headed to a local bar to try and forgot the sight of the insects back at the hotel.

As this was the time of year that summer dated trains operated, there was only one place to be and that's Namur. We all managed to get up in time to catch the 07.15 Brussels Midi to Milan with 2004. We easily made the 08.25 Namur to Houyet with 5302 and 5201 working in Top and Tail mode and took them to Dinant.

Left: •5302 at Dinant with the 08.25 from Namur
Right: 5201 at Dinant on the rear of the train with 5302.

From Dinant, we all headed back north by taking an EMU back to Namur then required 2302 to Charleroi whilst working the 10.05 Namur to Paris. After Charleroi we headed to Gent St Pieters to check out the diesels working there. Then back south to stay two nights at the Queen Vic.

The following day it was a summer Saturday, so off to the Ardennes it was. After breakfast it was straight onto the 08.25 departure which had •5320 on the rear and was taken down to Houyet. Then 5403 top and tailed with 5212 on the 08.46 Libramont to Dinant. For the same pair with 5212 leading on the 10.43 Dinant to Libramont as far as Bertrix then finally with 5403 leading on the 10.43 from Dinant across to Libramont.

Left: •5320 after arrival at Houyet on the 17th July 1999.
Right: 5212 prior to departing Dinant on the 17th July 1999.

From Libramont we headed north to the city of Brugge and took Monceau (Charleroi) allocated Class 51: 5148 from Brugge to Gent St Pieters whilst working the 18.56 Blankenberge to Maubeuge (France) summer dated service. Then straight back down to Namur for an evening in various bars in the town.

As the next day was a Sunday, we decided to head from Namur to Luxembourg, not via the direct route but via Koln, Germany. We headed east from Namur to Liege then onto Aachen to purchase a Schones Wochenende ticket. This ticket allowed up to five adults to travel freely for the whole weekend on most regional trains other than Inter City services in Germany.

Next, we all boarded the 10.14 Koln Deutz to Trier regional service with diesel 215.079 from Koln HBF to Gerolstein, where we took a short break in a nearby bar. We continued south to Trier with 215.040 working the 12.19 Gerolstein to Trier arriving in time to board the 15.47 Trier to Luxembourg with DB electric 181.209 which was taken to Wasserbillig where we purchased our CFL Day Rover tickets for onward travel to Luxembourg City. Our final train of the day was 181.224 whilst working a DB IR service: 09.15 Cuxhaven to Luxembourg. Then a swift walk to introduce my friends to Johnny at the hotel Carlton. As always, he was the perfect host and welcomed us all as if we were long lost friends.

That evening we visited a lovely Italian restaurant only to discover that Derek supposedly didn't like Italian food including Pasta and Pizza meals. After a little arm twisting, we managed to get him to order a dish of Ravioli as his mother had years ago given him a tin of Ravioli, which he vaguely remembered. The rest of us ordered various Pizza and pasta dishes. Siobhan ordered a Calzone which to all intense and purpose is a Pizza that has been folded to form what looks like a huge pasty. Well, when this arrived, Derek's eye just lit up. To make matters worse, Siobhan only fancied a small portion of the Calzone and gave up. Immediately, Derek, who had argued with us that he did not like pizza, grabbed the Calzone and demolished it in minutes. Needless to say, we gave him some real grief and told him in future not to be so difficult when it came to eating out with the rest of us.

The next day after an enjoyable breakfast, myself Bod and Derek spent the day covering as many local services as possible, whilst Sheila and Siobhan explored the city, especially the old quarter of the city, which by then had become a UNESCO world heritage site. The boys didn't have time for such things and with the aid of their cheap Rover Tickets were soon into their stride.

Left: 1817 departs Bettembourg with 06.30 Rodange to Luxembourg.
Right: 3603 at Wesserbillig with the 11.27 to Rodange.

During the course of the day, we managed to have 18 different engines including examples from Luxembourg, Germany and France. Luxembourg was really a superb place to bash and hopefully my friends enjoyed the place as much as myself. We finished the day off with an out and back from Luxembourg to Bettembourg with SNCF Class 16000: 16593 working the 18.30 to Metz and returned behind an SNCF Class 15000: 15062 whilst working the 18.04 from Metz. The

SNCF Class 16000, were known as Shoe Boxes, owing to their simple square shape design or lack of it!

Left: SNCF 16593 at Bettembourg
Right: CFL 3609 arrives at Cento Hamm, 17.27 from Wesserbillig.

The following day the 20th July was spent locally before taking SNCB 5510 working the 18.13 Luxembourg to Liege, where we stayed for two nights at the Univers Hotel.

On Wednesday the 21st July, we opted to split and go in different directions, whilst myself and Sheila would go back to Luxembourg via Namur to have required •5216 working the 11.05 Dinant to Houyet, whilst 5201 and 5403 were working in top and tail mode on the 10.43 Dinant to Libramont. From here we headed back to Namur then down to Luxembourg. The final out and back to Bettembourg involved SNCF 26045 out for SNCF 16695 back to Luxembourg City then SNCB diesel 5523 working the 18.13 Luxembourg to Liege, which we did throughout to Liege. Thursday 22nd July started with myself and Derek covering a few of the early morning rush hour services, including a run behind •5502 working the 05.10 Gouvy to Liers then •5507 working the 06.19 Gouvy to Liers.

Left: •5507 at Liege Guillemins with the 06.19 from Gouvy.
Right: •5407 at Houyet with the 10.51 Dinant to Houyet.

After going back to the hotel to enjoy breakfast, we were soon on our way heading west to Namur and down to the Ardennes for more Nohab action. We finally ended the day back at Liege and spent the evening in a local bar, which is where I heard the Cure for the first time. One of the bar staff was a huge fan of the Cure and kept playing their 'Disintegration' album, which I immediately bought once I got home. This was our last night in Liege before we moved back to Namur for the last two nights of the trip during which we managed to pick up •5306 10.51 Dinant to Houyet on the Friday before heading up to Gent St Pieters to have two SNCB Class 51s: 5141 working the 18.43 Blankenberge to Neerpelt and 5109 working the 20.09 Eeklo to Gent St Pieters. Then back to the Queen Vic and time for beer.

Saturday 24th July, would be the last full day of the trip and the morning was spent covering all three services on the Kayak's. First it was 5403 with •5313 on the rear working the 08.25 Namur to Houyet. At Houyet, I managed to persuade the Guard to allow us all to travel back to Dinant on the ECS with required •5313. At Dinant we took required •5214 on the 10.43 Dinant to Libramont. Unfortunately, on arrival at Bertrix SNCB decided to replace the Nohab and coaches with a pair of single car DMU's i.e., 4407 and 4508, which had to be taken across to Libramont.

Left: From left to right Bod, Siobhan, Derek, Sheila and myself, posing in front of •5313 at Dinant.
Right: •5214 at Dinant with the 10.43 to Libramont (Bertrix)

Another trip up to Brugge to cover dud 5148 working the 18.56 Blankenberge to Maubeuge, which was taken to Gent St Pieters then SNCB 2004 working the 19.25 Blankenberge to Arlon, which delivered us back to Namur. We spent the last night of the trip in a Brasserie close to the Queen Vic and hopefully a good time was had by all.

Sunday the 25th July, was our last day and involved a last trip up to Brussels where we took time out to visit some of the famous sights in the City centre.

Left and Right: The Grand Place, Brussels.

By 20.05 we had all somehow managed to board our BA flight back to Manchester, which brought to an end a fairly comprehensive visit to three countries. I suspect that Siobhan and Sheila weren't too excited with all the train travel but we did manage to squeeze a lot in.

Just to prove we did actually make it to the coast at Blankenberge. The author flashing his knees!

10 – Germany and the European Report

Whilst on a trip to Belgium, a couple of friends decided to make their first visit to Germany during a weekend. They opted to share a DB Schones Wochenende ticket, which in hindsight might not have been the best option. However, their experience persuaded me to make a similar trip during June 1997.

It was about this time I started to receive copies of the 'European Report' which was an excellent booklet produced by Mick Dunn, Phil Hodgson and Phil Wormald and cost in the region of £15 a year and was an invaluable part of bashing across Europe in those days.

Left: European Report Issue No 162, May 1997
Right: The German 1999 Timetable or Kursbuch. Including repairs.

The European Report comprised a number of sections including: Stock alterations, News, Sightings and interesting workings listed by individual countries and finally trip reports submitted by various European Bashers. The trip reports came in a similar format that listed a person's moves by each day of the trip. The report detailed the engines that the person travelled behind, the service that it was working plus the journey details i.e., where you boarded and exited plus the distance travelled. One of the most useful parts of trip reports was a list of hotels and B&B places individuals stayed plus contact details, cost of the rooms and an independent assessment of what the place was like. Not forgetting this at a time well before Booking.Com arrived, in fact even before the Internet happened. So, booking places to stay was challenging to say the least.

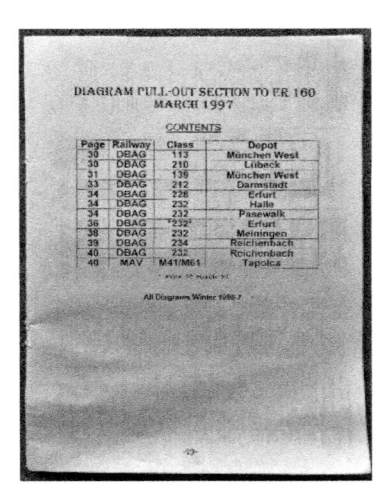

Left: The Dossers Guide produced by Jon Hayes
Right: The European Report – Diagram Pull Out.

Included within the European Report was a regular Diagram Pull Out Pamphlet, which detailed the diagrams for a class of engines listed on the front page. The diagrams were regularly obtained by either the authors or in some case individuals when they visited depots during their trips. The diagrams became a hugely important piece of gen that detailed how many engines were required from a particular depot. For example, on the Diagram Pull Out shown, it details the Darmstadt 212 diagrams commonly known as 'Coat Hangers'. These at the time comprised fourteen Monday to Friday diagrams covering services around Offenbach, Ober Roden, Frankfurt and Dieburg etc plus an additional weekday diagram for services around Worms.

Left: 212.361 departs Oberthausen: 13.07 Offenbach to Ober Roden
Right: 212.054 at Offenbach with the 13.05 from Ober Roden.

The German Timetable or Kursbuch was a fairly hefty book to carry around and you had no option other than carry it as there was no on-line timetabling system or Apps on your phone. DB then decided to change from a single book format to a series of books covering different areas of the country which fitted neatly in to a large cardboard box. However, the new format did help as it allowed you to just carry those books for the areas you intended to travel within. When a new Kursbuch was published you had to try and obtain one as soon as possible to see if any changes to the timetable would affect any future plans. Consequently, when anyone visited Germany soon after a new Kursbuch had been published, they were often persuaded to bring back extra copies, needless to say this was a considerable physical challenge. I'm sure Robin Havenhand remembers this challenge far too well!

Back to my first trip to Germany, which I planned to happen during one of my trips to Belgium during June 1997. I flew out to Brussels on Wednesday evening 25th June and stayed in Belgium to cover the Kayaks on the Saturday morning, which to be honest was a complete waste of time as none of the Nohab's were required. However, later in the day I did manage by pure luck to drop on former SNCB Class 60: 6077 which was working a PFT special from Virton close to the French border to Brussels Midi. Whilst, I had just arrived at Gembloux station on the 19.02 Blankenberge to Arlon summer dated service when the Class 60 rolled in on the opposite platform. This resulted in a quick exit and I was soon sat on the special which was taken to Ottignies, after which I continued my journey to Namur.

Left: a view of SNCB Class 60: 6077 from the first coach.
Right: 6077 (aka 210077) at Ottignies on the 28th June 1997.

The following day I had to do the 07.10 EMU departure from Namur to get me to Liege in time to board 06.34 Ostende to Koln HBF service with SNCB 2756. This delivered me to Aachen, where I visited the ticket Office to purchase a Schones Wochenende ticket. After a quick phot of my first German engine, which from now will be referred to as Loks, I was soon on my way to Koln HBF with 111.165 working the 09.12 Aachen to Bielefeld. Needless to say, I was very impressed with the main station at Koln and the magnificent sight of the Cathedral alongside the station. Koln HBF was a very busy station with virtually every train hauled and hardly a DMU or EMU in sight. First move was to do a quick out and back to Koln Sud on a couple of DB Class 215s working the semi fast service to Gerolstein and included 215.134 out for 215.136 back to Koln HBF.

Left: DB Class 111: 111.136 with the 09.03 to Hagen
Right: 215.134 departs Koln Sud with the 10.08 Koln HBF to Gerolstein.

Next, I was on a service to Koln Deutz station, which involved my first ever trip over the river Rhine via the famous Hohenzollern Bridge. The bridge contains six tracks and handles in excess of 1200 trains per day. Since that first visit, I will have crossed the bridge many hundreds of times. At Koln Deutz I took my first DB Class 218 (aka Rabbit) 218.132 to a place called Rosrath on the 11.03 Koln Hansaring to Gummersbach. It wasn't long before I was on my second Rabbit with 218.131 working the 10.40 Gummersbach to Koln Hansaring.

Left: 218.132 departs Rosrath with a service to Gummersbach.
Right: 218.131 after arrival back at Koln HBF.

After dozens of crossings of the river Rhein on various classes including: 110s, 111s, 141s, 143s, 215s and 218s it was time to head to Essen HBF to cover the DB Class 216s working the services from Wuppertal Oberbarmen to Bottrop and Haltern West and on that day included: 216.028, 216.083, 216.091, 216.152, 216.155 & 216.157 plus the odd spin behind some DB Class 143s fondly known as 'Trabbies' (aka Trabants the former East German built car)

Left: 216.091 at Essen West, 15.22 Wuppertal Oberbarmen to Bottrop. Right: 216.157 with the 17.51Bottrop to Langenberg.

I don't think I had every covered so many trains in one day and by 18.40 pm I was heading from Essen to Aachen to exit Germany back to Belgium. The following day was the last day of the trip and I flew back on the 20.10 BA service from Brussels to Manchester on G-BGDA a B737-200 series.

On reflection, I should definitely have spent the whole weekend in Germany as the Kayaks were a complete waste of time but that's life. That first trip to Germany certainly fired up my imagination and I was quickly into planning my second visit to the country. This was helped when BA started to operate flights direct from Manchester to Dusseldorf at an affordable price.

The plan was to fly from Manchester to Dusseldorf on Wednesday 20th August and return from Brussels on Tuesday 26th August 1997. For my travel in Germany, I purchased a DB Regional rover ticket that offered 5 days unlimited travel on all DB passenger services. I bought the Rover Ticket at Dusseldorf Flugh and it covered an area bounded by Dortmund, Aachen, Saarbrucken, Mannheim, Frankfurt, Siegen and back to Dortmund. The ticket cost the equivalent of £59 whatever that was in Deutsche Mark. Similar tickets existed for different areas of Germany and one of the most popular tickets covered an area that previously was East Germany. There were stories that some bashers used these tickets as if they were a German All line Rover ticket, just rumours but believable.

After my arrival at Dusseldorf, I headed down to Koln and stayed the night at the Staplehauschen Hotel alongside the River Rhein, which I had found by contacting the German Tourist Board in Koln. The hotel would become a frequent base for me when staying on the Ruhr and simply was an ideal place to stay with its obvious history.

The following day the hotel owner provided a fabulous breakfast including my first ever Kiwi fruit. I suspect breakfast would normally have been available at a much later time but as I had told the owner I needed to be on an early train, they prepared a breakfast just for myself, which was very much appreciated.

Left: The Hotel Staplehauschen viewed from the banks of the Rhein.
Right: 103.203 at the buffer stops at Frankfurt HBF

After a fabulous breakfast, I walked across to Koln HBF and located my Euro City service which had a DB Class 103: 103.218, my first DB Class 103 for haulage. The service was the 05.54 Koln HBF to Wien and I intended to take it all the way to Frankfurt HBF, no short leap on your first 103 for haulage allowed! The Class 103s had been for some time, Germany's top link Inter City lok and totalled 145 plus four prototypes. By 1997 a dozen or so of the class had been withdrawn, usually as a result of major crash damage. So, the challenge was to see how many of the remaining examples (approx. 130) you could have before DB started mass withdrawals of the class following the introduction of the Class 101s and Inter City ICE trains.

On arrival at Frankfurt HBF, I hoped to board the 08.14 to Stuttgart HBF, which was booked to be hauled by a Darmstadt Class 215. The connection at Frankfurt was extremely tight and thankfully I noticed the Stuttgart service in the bay platform alongside platform 1 as my train arrived. So, after a manic sprint around to the bay platform, which also involved me shouting at the guard to hold the train, I somehow managed to make the back coach and jumped on as the guard shut the doors. Suspect, if that was today I would have well and truly missed the train!

Left: 215.141 departs Gross Umstadt with the service from Frankfurt.
Right: 215.144 at Darmstadt with the 10.44 to Eberbach.

After a number of moves on Class 215s, I took 215.101 whilst working the 09.05 Stuttgart HBF to Frankfurt HBF as far as Offenbach to cover the Darmstadt 212s diagrams. These included in the order they worked: 212.361, 212.054, 212.052, 212.371 and 212.038. Then direct to Frankfurt HBF in time for the afternoon rush hour Class 216 departures on the services to Stockheim and Nidda, which included 216.120, 216.222 paired with 216.191, 216.203, 216.197 and finally 216.196.

Left: 216.120 with the 16.45 Frankfurt HBF to Stockheim at Frankfurt.
Right: 216.197 at Bad Vibel with the 18.45 Frankfurt HBF to Nidda.

After the Class 216s it was time to enjoy a couple of Class 103s between Frankfurt and Mainz, the place I had booked to stay that night. First, it was the turn of 103.213 working 08.18 Budapest to Dortmund to Mainz. Then I walked to the hotel to check-in and found a place to eat and enjoy the odd beer. After which, I took 103.120 on the 12.26 Westerland to Nurnberg, back to Frankfurt and finally 110.389 working the 14.20 Wien to Koln EC service, with arrival at Mainz at around 22.30 pm, surprisingly a DB 110 on an EC service!

The next day Friday 22nd August 1997, I viewed 218.368 at Mainz HBF on the 05.07 to Saarbrucken but my plan would take me back to Koln on the 04.41 Frankfurt HBF to Dortmund IC with 103.168. Then 103.237 forward from Koln to Dusseldorf HBF on the 07.09 Koln HBF to Amsterdam Centraal EC. Yes, in the days when loco hauled trains still operated to Amsterdam. At Dusseldorf, I covered two booked Class 212 diagrams, the first produced 212.297 working the 06.58 Wuppertal HBF to Dusseldorf HBF, whilst the second was 212.283 working the 07.44 Remscheid Lennep to Dusseldorf HBF. After the Coat Hangers I heading up to Duisburg HBF to cover two Class 215 diagrams on the service to Xanten. These included 215.094 working the 10.04 to Xanten which was taken to Moers for 215.073 working the 10.06 Xanten to Duisburg. 215.073 was a modified version of the class that had exhaust ports similar to their bigger brothers the Class 218 which were known as Rabbits, so the 215s with these types of Exhaust were known as Baby Bunnies!

Left: 215.095 at Dusseldorf HBF with the 09.19 to Kleeve.
Right: 215.073 at Rheinhausen with the 10.06 Xanten to Duisburg HBF

Next destination was Essen for a four hour visit to cover all the Class 216 diagrams plus numerous Trabbies. During my stay I managed the get the following 216s in the order they worked: 216.026, 216.155, 216.091, 216.152, 216.146, 216.083, 216.154, 216.026 again, 216.093 and finally 216.161, an impressive haul for only my second visit!

Left: 216.146 at Essen HBF with the 13.39 Langenberg to Bottrop.
Right: 216.083 departs Essen West with the 14.11 from Bottrop.

Soon after 16.00 pm I departed Essen on 103.233 working the 12.33 Hamburg Altona to Koln HBF as far as Duisburg HBF before taking 103.187 on the 14.12 Hamburg Altona to Koln HBF through to its destination. My final move was an out and back to Koln Sud to get 215.047 out for 215.035 on the return, both working Gerolstein services. I left Koln HBF and headed west to Namur where I was staying the night. I took SNCB 1801 from Koln HBF working the 20.14 Koln HBF to Ostende to Liege Guillemins then a SNCB Break EMU from Liege to Namur and headed straight to the Queen Vic.

The reason for heading back to Namur was the following day was a Summer Saturday, so it was time for some Nohab action on the Kayaks. First of all, required •5209 worked the 08.25 Namur to Houyet then I had required •5304 with •5311 on the rear working the 08.32 Libramont to Dinant. As •5311 wasn't working on the rear, resulted in a move down to Bertrix with •5311 working the 10.30 Dinant to Bertrix. Then a series of moves to get me across to Liege for another crossing into Germany via Aachen, one might say a flying visit to Belgium but that was the way things happened back then.

Left: •5209 at Namur with the 08.25 to Houyet.
Right: •5311 at Dinant prior to working the 10.30 to Bertrix.

By about 16.50, I was heading north from Koln HBF on required 103.135 working the 13.22 Karlsruhe to Norddeich Mole as far as Dusseldorf HBF. At Dusseldorf I did a series of moves between there and Krefeld to slot in as many Dusseldorf allocated Class 215s as well as numerous Class 110s working around Krefeld.

The highlight of the evening was when the driver of 215.117 invited me to join him for the journey from Krefeld Oppum back to Dusseldorf HBF. It was only then I noticed that German loks had a wheel that allowed them to apply power from the engine as opposed to a power handle used on most diesel and electric locomotives in the UK.

First Photo: 215.117 at Krefeld HBF: 19.06 Kleeve to Dusseldorf HBF.
Remaining Photos: inside the cab and the arrival at Dusseldorf HBF.

After all the excitement of the cab ride, I took required 103.217 north to Duisburg HBF then 110.105 from there back to Koln HBF and an end to a truly fantastic day. That night I stayed at the Staplehauschen again and took advantage of the local bars to enjoy some food and beers.

Sunday 24th August 1997, after another excellent breakfast, I was soon boarding a Class 215 at 07.17 am with an out and back to Koln Sud enabling me to have 215.038 for 215.036.

This was the start of an absolutely manic day which would eventually see me recording 52 different loks for haulage and an eventual finish at about 23.15 pm. The highlight of the day was when I was photographing 103.155 at Koln HBF whilst working the Inter Regional 07.22 Karlsruhe to Emden, only for the driver to invite me for another cab ride. The driver was Dutch and spoke fluent English, so no communication problems this time. He was being trained on the route prior to the introduction of modern ICE trains to Amsterdam. The incredible sound of the 103 as we departed Koln HBF was almost deafening but very impressive. He invited me to travel with him further north but my desire to scratch more loks won the day! truly shameful!!!!

Left: 103.155 Koln HBF whilst working the 07.22 Karlsruhe to Emden. Right: A view from the cab of 103.155 with another 103 about to pass at a closing speed in excess of 300 KPH.

The remaining day involved more than a dozen 103s plus more Class 215s around Koln before calling it a day soon after 23.15 pm.

The next day Monday 25th August, I headed down to Bonn to cover the Class 215 diagrams around there, before travelling further south to Koblenz to see which diesels were working to Giessen. Only 32 loks for haulage that day, so I was obviously easing off a little but that did include me exiting Germany once again as I headed back over to Namur to stay at the Queen Vic. I just can't think why I decided to book a flight out of Brussels as a return from Dusseldorf would have been far more convenient. The benefits of Hindsight!!!!

Left: 216.221 at Koblenz with the 12.14 to Giessen.
Right: 215.116 at a shack on the line from Euskirchen to Bonn.

Tuesday 26th August was the last day of the trip and involved covering lots of P trains including in the order they worked: 2370, 2615, 2325, 2510, 2316 and 5118, unfortunately all dud. It was only when I headed down to Leuven to cover the 16.15 to Dendermonde that massive •5125 came to my rescue. I took this to Mechelen then I scored 2231 before heading to the airport for my BA flight back to Manchester with G-BKYO - B737-200 series.

Monster SNCB •5125 at Leuven prior to working the 16.15.

After the August trip, I had one further trip during September which involved flying to Belgium then onto Luxembourg and Germany.

By December I must have started to get itchy feet, and had a chat with friends Andy Read and Robin Havenhand about the possibility of a joint trip over the Christmas holiday period. The discussion resulted in flight being booked involving flying out from Manchester on the 27th December and returning home on the 30th December 1997. This was Robins first trip to Germany and it certainly opened up his eyes to a whole new world. Andy had been to Germany before and his previous experience certainly helped us during this short 4-day trip. Myself and Robin flew from Manchester to Dusseldorf and by 10.35 am we had purchased our Regional Rovers and were on our way to

Dusseldorf HBF. By the end of the day, we had slotted in a total of 33 loks for haulage and managed to book into a Best Western Hotel close to Mainz HBF for two nights. Here we found time for a meal and the odd beer before finishing the day off with a few short leaps on two Trabbies and 141.232, which was taken to Wiesbaden.

Left: 215.014 at Krefeld with the 12.06 Kleeve to Dusseldorf HBF.
Right: 216.034 at Essen HBF with the 14.54 Haltern to Wuppertal Ob.

By 07.00 am the next day, we were heading down to Bensheim on 103.114 whilst working the 06.03 Koblenz to Karlsruhe IC service. Then it was time for some Darmstadt 215s during which time I managed to score 215.063 and 215.143 before heading to an area to the west of Mainz to cover a number of Kaiserslautern 218 diagrams. This included, in the order they worked: 218.370, 218.371, 218.378, 218.361 and 218.363. At the time loks in Germany came in a variety of colour schemes including: Blue and white, Old Rot (A dark Red), new Rot, Green and Black, Dark Blue and Black plus Orange and White, which certainly gave some variety to our photographs.

Left: 215.143 at Hetschbach with the 10.40 Darmstadt to Erbach
Right: 218.378 at Bad Kreuznach with the 15.47 to Mainz HBF.

We finished the day with a couple of 103s: 103.131 12.36 Westerland to Nurnberg from Mainz HBF to Frankfurt Flugh then 103.205 14.20 Wien to Koln HBF back to Mainz HBF.

The next day would be our last full day of the trip and we had to be back at Koln at the end of the day, ready for our return flights on the 30th December. So, we spent the morning covering the Darmstadt 212 diagrams, which included: 212.053, 212.357, 212.049, 212.358, 212.361, 212.025, 212.355, 212.051 and finally 212.030.

Left: 212.358 at Ober Roden with the 09.07 from Offenbach.
Right: 212.030 at Offenbach HBF with the 11.51 from Dieburg.

Andy suggested we head from Frankfurt north to Giessen to check out the diesels. This wasn't in the original plan but turned out to be an excellent idea. Virtually all the local services in and out of Giessen were still diesel hauled including Class 212s and 216s with just the odd 628 DMU spoiling a perfect day. After having twelve different diesels for haulage, we finished our visit to Giessen with 216.205 from Giessen to Limburg whilst working the 17.51 Giessen to Limburg then forward to Koblenz with 216.223 on the 18.30 Giessen to Koblenz.

Left: 216.143 at Friedberg with the 14.16 to Giessen.
Right: 216.192 departs Grossen Buseck with the 15.12 from Giessen.

The diesels at Giessen included in the order they worked: 216.143, 212.095, 212.072, 216.192, 216.101, 216.217, 216.203, 216.058, 216.185, 216.205, 216.223 plus 216.193 at Friedberg (Hess). Needless to say, a thoroughly good afternoon was had by all. We took 103.175 working the 09.12 Budapest to Dortmund EC from Koblenz to Koln HBF, where we just couldn't resist a quick out and back to Koln Deutz with 218.148 out for 215.052 back to Koln HBF.

We then checked into hotel very close to the station and managed to get a triple room for our last night.

Tuesday 30th December 1997, as this was the last day of our trip, we wouldn't let that stop us spinning around the Ruhr. First plan was to cover three Koln Class 212 diagrams that arrived in Dusseldorf HBF during the morning rush hour. By soon after 08.30 we had bagged 212.270 06.27 Wuppertal Oberbarmen to Dusseldorf HBF, followed by 212.319 06.58 Wuppertal HBF to Dusseldorf HBF and finally 212.328 07.43 Remscheid Lennep to Dusseldorf HBF.

The rest of the day was spent on the Ruhr covering as much as possible, including two more Baby Bunnies: 215.079 and 215.081 and last but not least my first DB Class 151: 151.060 whilst working the 16.13 Koln HBF to Wuppertal Oberbarmen rush hour services. These electrics would usually work freights but some would find themselves working passenger services during a rush hour period.

Left: 215.081 at Duisburg after arrival with the 12.06 from Xanten.
Right: 151.060 Koln HBF with the 16.13 to Wuppertal Oberbarmen.

By 20.00 pm, myself and Robin were back at Dusseldorf Flugh in time for the 20.25 BA flight to Manchester, with required G-BGDG doing the honours. This brought to an end another thoroughly enjoyable trip, considerably helped by having two friends for company. By now Germany had become my number one country to bash and slowly but surely visits to other countries just got put on the back burner. The country was huge and had a massive rail network and that was even before I summoned up the courage to venture in to the former East Germany.

However, before my first visit to East Germany I still had loads of exploring to do within the former West Germany. My next long trip started on Saturday 4th April and lasted until my return on Easter Sunday 12th April 1998. On the Saturday morning I flew from Manchester on the 07.00 BA flight to Brussels and immediately headed over to Germany, arriving in Aachen by 13.00 pm. I must have bought a Schones Wochenende ticket as I made no effort to board any Inter City services during the weekend. I stayed at the Staplehauschen, Koln for two nights and used it as a base.

During the weekend I covered over fifty local services on the Ruhr and only once had a 103 which was 103.182 whilst working the 08.59 Koln Deutz to Eindhoven, which only involved a trip across the Rhein from Deutz to Koln HBF. I managed to pick a couple of Class 140s plus loads of Class 215s and 216s.

Left: 103.182 at Koln Deutz with the 08.59 to Eindhoven.
Right: 140.534 at Koln HBF with the 10.13 to Koblenz on the Sunday.

By Monday 6th April my DB Regional Rover ticket started which allowed me to travel on Inter City services. However, the first services to cover were the Koln Class 212 diagrams arriving at Dusseldorf, so I headed across to Solingen Ohligs to cover these and managed 212.234 and 212.255 but must have missed 212.266 which I viewed arrive at Solingen Ohligs with an ECS. At least, two is better than none.

Left: 212.266 at Solingen Ohligs with an ECS.

After the Coat Hangers it was time to cover as many services as possible along the Ruhr corridor including dozens of 103s. which included winners: 103.158, 103.191, 103.108, 103.217, 103.164, 103.154, 103.210, 103.132, 103.231, 103.190, 103.241 and finally 103.117. Thankfully I decided to cover the afternoon rush hour at Koln HBF and was rewarded with 151.037, 151.048 and 215.029.

Left: 151.037 with the 16.13 Koln HBF to Wuppertal Oberbarmen. Right: 215.029 16.20 Koln Deutz to Bedburg.

The bash became somewhat frantic soon after 17.00 pm when 151.048 rolled into Koln HBF with the 17.13 departure to Wuppertal Oberbarmen then on the opposite side of the same island platform 155.233 arrived with the 17.13 to Koblenz, both stopping at Koln Deutz. Solution. Soultion, wait in the middle of the platform until the first train is given the green light then dive on the train. 151.048 was first and I managed to get on board but the train soon came to a halt on the bridge, resulting in 155.233 passing the train I was sat on. As soon as my train arrived at Deutz, I tried desperately to dive under the subway, down at least 40 steps then up another 40 steps to the platform that the 155 had stopped at. What a surprise the 155 had already set off when I arrived at the top of the steps, resulting in lots of cursing and swearing!!

After this disappointment, I headed south to Kaiserslautern where I had prebooked to stay at a local B&B. The plan was to cover some Kaiserslautern Class 212 diagrams in the morning. The B&B was a family run place and owing to my early start I was forced to miss breakfast.

Tuesday 7th April, I was on 05.31 Kaiserslautern to Pirmasens with 212.347 which I took to Steinalben for a 628 DMU back to Kaiserslautern. Next, it was 212.343 out to Niedermohr for 212.323 back to Landstuhl. During which time I missed 212.278 working the 07.06 Kaiserslautern to Kusel. The rest of the day I covered loads of Class 141s, 143s, 181s and 218s. I finished the day off at Mainz HBF doing four 10's on the bounce i.e., 103.218, 103.242, 103.207 and finally 103.218 again on short moves to Frankfurt Flugh. Not the most productive set of moves as I only scored 103.207!

Left: 212.323 at Landstuhl with the 06.44 Kusel to Kaiserslautern.
Right: 218.364 at Ingelheim with the 15.01 Tuerkismuehle to Mainz.

After staying at a hotel in Mainz it was time to cover the Darmstadt 212s before heading north to Giessen to spend the whole of the afternoon there. The 212 moves proved successful with five new including class leader: 212.001.

Left: Line up of 212's at Ober Roden 212.027, 212.367 and 212.023. Right; 212.001 at Ober Roden with the 11.07 arrival from Offenbach.

After taking required 212.367 to Offenbach, I headed north to Giessen, where I had pre-booked to stay at a local hotel. En route to Giessen, I covered a couple of 216s working off Friedberg (Hess), which included 216.136 and 216.101 and eventually arrived at Giessen on former DR electric 112.175 whilst working the 14.03 Frankfurt HBF to Munster IR service. These services were usually at the time hauled in top and tail mode with a 112 at either end, so don't know what happened to the other 112 that day, unless the sight of a 212 on stock caused me to forget about the other 112!

Consequently, my first move was an out and back to Grossen Buseck with 212.374 working 14.51 Giessen to Fulda for a return to Giessen with 212.104 working 13.31 Fulda to Giessen.

Left: 212.374 at Giessen with the 14.51 to Fulda.
Right 212.104 at Giessen after arriving with the 13.31 from Fulda.

Giessen, soon became one of my favourite places to visit during my trips to Germany. I suspect it wasn't much different from the day's when diesels were first introduced after the era of steam. By 19.30, I had managed to have 14 different loks for haulage, including one electric. The diesels included: 212.374, 212.104, 216.144, 216.145, 216.127, 216.212, 216.120, 216.139, 216.097, 216.222, 216.117, 216.116 and finally 216.127.

Left: 216.145 at Reiskirchen with the 15.46 Giessen to Fulda.
Right: 216.212 arrives at Grunberg with the 15.33 Fulda to Giessen, whilst 216.127 is ready to depart with the 16.12 Giessen to Alsfeld.

My hotel was fairly close to the station and for a change I finished at the relatively early time of 19.30 pm. The evening was spent in a local bar which thankfully served food. One other fond memory I have of Giessen was the opportunity to purchase freshly made Crepes from a mobile unit outside the station and needless to say they were very tasty!!

The next day was Thursday 9th April 1998 and I had decided to stay around Giessen until after the afternoon rush hour. This allowed me to cover a few electric diagrams including DB Class 110s, 112s, 140s, 141s and finally a 103. Two of the Munster to Frankfurt IR services were operating with 112s in top and tail mode and included: 112.108 & 112.114 as well as 112.144 & 112.175. I also managed to have two DB Class 140s: 140.757 and 140.817. During my stay, I bumped into a very pleasant young female guard who was obviously pleased to meet someone from the UK and she gave me a large chocolate Rabbit as an Easter present.

Left: 140.817 at Giessen with the 12.19 Dillenburg to Kassel.
Right: 216.165 at Giessen with the 13.21 to Alsfeld.

I was lucky once again to drop on two Class 212s, working the same trains as yesterday but this time with two new loks. First, I took 212.293 working the 14.51 Giessen to Fulda to Grossen Buseck for 212.287 working the 13.31 Fulda to Giessen. I suspect these two services must have been diagrammed for Coat Hangers at the time.

Left: 212.293 at Giessen with the 14.51 to Fulda
Right: 212.287 at Giessen after arriving with the 13.31 from Fulda.

I covered virtually all the afternoons rush hour services and finished with a batch of moves behind 216s including: 216.143, 216.221, 216.217, 216.060 and finally 216.116 which was taken to Koblenz then straight onto 103.174 working the 09.18 Budapest to Dortmund EC service. I must have arrived at Koln HBF around 22.30, so headed straight to the Staplehauschen Hotel.

Friday 10th April 1998 – Good Friday. After another fabulous breakfast at the hotel, I walked over to Koln HBF and fell on required 103.130 working the 06.39 Koln HBF to Emden, which I took to Dusseldorf. Then 103.215 from Dusseldorf to Duisburg with the 08.09 Koln HBF to Westerland.

At Duisburg HBF I was pleased to see preserved V200.116 working a Rheingold Express charter service.

Left: 103.130 at Koln HBF with one of DB new ICE trains alongside.

This was the last day of my Regional Rover, so made the most of travelling behind Class 103s and finished the day with thirteen new 103s including: 103.130, 103.215, 103.180, 103.221, 103.126, 103.188, 103.102, 103.227, 103.169, 103.156, 103.138, 103.162 and finally 103.163.

Saturday 11th April 1998, I was again using a Schones Wochenende ticket, which restricted me to Regional services. The first train of the day was a Trabbie: 143.619 working a S-Bahn service via Koln HBF, which I took to Koln

Hansaring S-Bahn station then straight back to Koln HBF only to see 151.085 arrive on the 06.38 Wuppertal Oberbarmen to Koln HBF service! Doh!! Soon after, V200.116 worked another Rheingold Express service departing Koln HBF soon after 07.30 am. The rest of the day was spent along the Ruhr valley and included a run behind Coat Hanger: 212.050 from Krefeld HBF to Dusseldorf HBF whilst working the 14.06 Kleeve to Dusseldorf HBF. I did manage to sneak in a couple of trips behind 103s during the day, although one was 103.157 whilst working the 17.08 Koln Deutz to Eindhoven and only involved a bridge crossing of the river Rhein from Deutz to Koln HBF, so I managed to avoid any Grippers.

Easter Sunday 12th April 1998, the last day of the trip and I had to be back at Brussels Airport for the 20.00 BA flight to Manchester. As a consequence, I spent the morning around Koln HBF before taking 111.120: 07.52 Bielefeld to Aachen, a 10.50 departure from Koln HBF across to Aachen.

Then onto SNCB Class 16: 1605 whilst working the 11.14 Koln HBF to Ostende EC service, which was taken to Brussels. Then onto the airport for my flight home, this time with BA G-BGDT B737-200 series and the end of another successful trip to Germany.

Why I flew via Brussels, must have been decided purely on cost grounds, as obviously it would have been much more convenient and productive for me to have flown directly to Dusseldorf from Manchester.

DB 120.130 passing Koln Deutz station with a south bound EC service with the magnificent Koln Cathedral (aka Dom) in the back ground.

That brings to an end a fairly comprehensive review of the period 1986 until 1997 when I had well and truly got the bug for railways abroad. The next book will continue with my visits to Germany and the eventual move into the former East Germany plus visits to a number of new countries including: Czech Republic, Slovakia and Hungary.

I hope you've found this book interesting and for some of you, rekindled fond memories for those who like myself have a love affair with anything to do with railways, whether that be at home or abroad.

Printed in Great Britain
by Amazon